NIALL O'DOWD
An Irish Voice

'A classic work of emigrant literature which, in the Irish canon, deserves to be assessed alongside such works such as Patrick McGill's *Children of the Dead End* and Donal MacAmhlaigh's *Diallan Diorat* or, in the American, with Barack Obama's *Dreams from My Father*.'

Tim Pat Coogan, Irish Independent

'An extraordinary story ... remarkably candid. O'Dowd's vision for the peace process has guaranteed him a place in the history books.'

The Belfast Telegraph

'Remarkable ... riveting political reportage'

The Irish Times

'A valuable contribution to the history of the peace process as well as the Irish emigrant experience. Niall's is a powerful story and it may well yet prove to be a classic of the emigrant genre.'

Taoiseach Brian Cowen

'highly readable... a worthy contribution to the literature on emigration and an insightful exploration of the relationship between Ireland and the US.'

Phoenix Magazine

'At times painfully honest, at other times wittily self-effacing, this is O'Dowd's account of his times as an undocumented Irishman working in the US ... a witty and lively book, and a hopeful one.'

The Sunday Tribune

'unflinchingly recounts the Irish immigrant experience of the 1980s ... a story familiar to Irish emigrants the world over, yet rarely is it written about so candidly. The book is fluid and dynamic, the story remarkable. You can detect the influence of American writers like Hemingway and Whitman. O'Dowd shares a similarly pure and eloquent writing voice: deceptively simple, but an art in itself.'

The Huffington Post

NIALL O'DOWD is the author of *Fire in the Morning,* about the Irish at the World Trade Centre on 9/11, founder of *Irish America* magazine, *Irish Voice* newspaper and IrishCentral.com, and an adjunct professor of journalism at Columbia University. A native of Ireland, he lives in New York.

NIALL
O'DOWD

AN IRISH VOICE

THE O'BRIEN PRESS
DUBLIN

This edition first published 2010 by The O'Brien Press Ltd,
12 Terenure Road East, Rathgar, Dublin 6, Ireland.
Tel: +353 1 4923333; Fax: +353 1 4922777
E-mail: books@obrien.ie
Website: www.obrien.ie
Original edition published 2010 by The O'Brien Press Ltd.

ISBN: 978-1-84717-223-5

A catalogue record for this title is available from the British Library

2 3 4 5 6 7 8 9 10
10 11 12 13 14 15 16

Front cover photograph by Kit DeFever
Picture section photographs and back cover photograph supplied by the author.

Printed and bound in the UK by J F Print Ltd, Sparkford, Somerset.
The paper in this book is produced using pulp from managed forests.

Dedication

To Donal and Kathleen

Acknowledgements

Thank you to the many people who made this book possible: my colleagues at *Irish Voice* newspaper, *Irish America* magazine and IrishCentral.com; Michael O'Brien of The O'Brien Press for believing in the project, Mary Webb, for her patience and talent as my editor; and my wife Debbie and daughter Alana for their support always.

Contents

Inside Obama's White House	09
A Soldier in Hillary's Losing Battle	13
The Wisdom of Bill	22
How Hillary Earned Her Spurs	26
My Father's Dream	32
California Here I Come	36
San Francisco Dreaming	48
The City of Broad Shoulders	53
The Leavetaking	56
Not So Welcome To America	63
Trying to Fit In	72
Building Site Blues	78
Animal House and Falling in Love	84
Go West Young Man	98
A Death in the Family	102
Return to America	108
Starting a Newspaper	115
Publisher and Chief Bottlewasher	120
Irish 1, Moonies 0	131
Farewell to Jennie	134
Friends or Lovers?	136
A Political Awakening	141
Tough Times in San Francisco	150
A Texas Friend in Need	163
Go East Young Man	166
Into the Darkness	172
A Man of Two Countries	181
The Irish Voice	190

Tackling the Northern Question 195

Getting Bill Clinton on Board 207

Clinton Wins the White House 214

Setting the Scene 221

Gathering Pace 232

Completing the A-Team 241

Ready to Go 246

A Dangerous Journey 250

Into the Cauldron 256

Prelude to a Visa 263

The Visa Battle 266

The San Diego Incident 272

The Media Go Wild 280

Adams Arrives 284

A Rock Star Reception 287

Tough Words at the White House 293

Waiting for the Ceasefire 296

IRA Breakdown 303

9/11 and the Aftermath 307

Battling for the Undocumented Irish 311

Irish Central Launches 315

Chapter 1

INSIDE OBAMA'S WHITE HOUSE

When you step into the White House it is an extraordinary experience. The immensity of the seat of power in the most powerful of all countries hits you with full force.

On the walls are arrayed the predecessors of Barack Obama, the man we have come to honour this night of 17 March, St Patrick's Day 2009. The fine china and cutlery from Jackie Kennedy's state dinner service lies within touch, mounted on the wall. The silver goblets that Andrew Jackson used at his state events in the 1830s are all present and accounted for. For a country that is so ambivalent about the general topic of history the American White House reeks of it.

And tonight we are witnessing a slice of history that John F Kennedy and Andrew Jackson, the old Indian hater, could only have dreamed of – though in Jackson's case it might have been a nightmare!

The first ever black president of the United States, Barack Obama, is holding court for the Irish in the house that kept Irish and blacks out for so long. The 'No Irish Need Apply' signs only came down in the lifetime of many present here tonight. And the idea of a black man as president was the stuff of pure fiction and bad jokes only a few years ago.

Yet here we are: one group who came as slaves, and so many of the other in coffin ships. This is our night, to celebrate with this young African American man who has capsized the stars.

On the way to the East Wing the crowds are moving slowly, taking in the significance of the occasion. Marines in their crisp dress uniforms stand by, ready at a second's notice to spring into action to help the guests.

Even the coat check is intriguing, once the site of the White House private cinema where Jack and Jackie watched movies, where George W. Bush invited Ted Kennedy soon after his inauguration to watch a film about the Cuban missile crisis. Little did he know that Kennedy hated to watch footage about his beloved brothers.

But that is the past and Kennedy is not here tonight, laid low by dreadful illness, a brain tumour that has brought the lion of the senate to his knees, and will cause his untimely death five months' later, on 25 August 2009. It is a shame, because he helped create tonight with his extraordinary support for Obama at a critical time in the primaries. That booming voice will not be heard tonight, and the event is a little poorer for its absence.

The guests stare at each other furtively. Who got on the list and who didn't is the great parlour game that has been resonating throughout the Irish American community for the past few weeks. But the Obama folk have focused heavily on their Chicago political friends, not necessarily Irish. That left many in the Irish American community out and very sore at the prospect.

Those of us who are there feel the rub of the green, the sigh of relief that we are still on the list. For others, including one Irish leader who stood outside, hoping that someone would shoo him in from the cold, it was a night to forget.

After we mount the stairs we are standing in the sweeping corridor walkway which connects the two parts of the East Wing. In the distance Hillary Clinton comes into view, alone, somehow vulnerable in the place she once called home and had hoped to do so again. She is Secretary of State, a powerful figure, but tonight she enters alone. We talk, as we always do. She asks about my family, I about hers. She remembers everyone's names, knows the issues, but you can tell also that she knows this is not her night. Before her conqueror arrives she slips away.

The band plays on as the guests gather, and soon President Obama and Michelle come striding down the corridor, accompanied by Taoiseach Brian Cowen and his wife Mary. It is, in the best sense of the phrase, 'a sight to behold'.

President Obama in person is remarkably slight, thin as a spindle. They say he will only play basketball in a track suit in order to hide his skinny legs. It is the smile that captivates, however, the broad flashing megawatt grin that he uses so effectively when greeting everybody. His body language this night is very relaxed, very open. He is clearly among friends. The Chicago bosses gather round him like bees at a honeycomb. He is the biggest star in the universe and they know it.

Michelle is striking, much more so than he. She has the duskier complexion, reflecting her broader African roots. She is also the warmer of the two, grabbing people and hugging. He stands back and waits for people to come to him.

The President and Taoiseach speak twice, once in the East Room and once in the West Room in order to satisfy the 300 or so present. Obama is utterly at ease. He knows this crowd. He grew up with Irish pols in Chicago and many were his mentors. Somewhere in the audience, Chicago Mayor Richard Daley is smiling quietly. His father made JFK and now he has helped make Barack Obama.

And what a politician this president is. When Brian Cowen accidentally begins reading from Obama's speech on the autocue, he pretends to read from Cowen's speech when it is his turn, smoothing over the moment and utterly putting his guests at ease.

One of his close advisors told me that Obama wanted to move into the White House as soon as he could, so he could still remember what it was like to put the garbage out and have a normal household for his kids, before all the various staff took over the everyday duties of daily life. As an example of how distanced one can become in that sort of situation, Nancy Soderberg, who was Deputy National Security Advisor for President Clinton, told me she found it shocking when she had to hail her own cab instead of having a limousine fetch her from home the day after she left the White House.

Unlike previous occupants, Obama had never entered that bubble of being a governor where normal life fades and is replaced by a battery of worker bees ready to carry out your every whim, and he had not been a senator for very long.

This night he was happy. As he surveyed the room, that golden smile flashed again and again; he had made it and no one could take it away from him. We Irish certainly had no desire to. We loved seeing history being made and having an underdog rewrite it.

As for me, I reflected how, just a few months ago, I had been working very hard to defeat him. Not anymore, he was my president now too. But, honestly, I never thought it would happen.

Chapter 2

A SOLDIER IN HILLARY'S
LOSING BATTLE

'Niall, have you met Barack?' asked Senator Hillary Clinton, taking me by the arm. We were in the ballroom of the Mayflower Hotel in Washington. It was July 2008 and the presidential election had entered its decisive stage.

Against all the odds, the first-time Senator from Illinois had defeated the heavy favourite, Hillary Clinton, who I had avidly supported for the Democratic nomination. Now we were all playing the good guy game, her key supporters meeting for the first time with the young man who had overturned our world, all in the name of Democratic unity.

Though the flesh was willing, the spirit was weak. Everyone seemed ill at ease. Even Obama himself lacked the radiant presence we had come to expect. When Hillary addressed us, he stood with arms folded, eyes fixed in the middle distance, betraying all in his body language. For Hillary, this moment was an especially tough blow. Yet she had soldiered on through so many crises in her life that she bore this one bravely too. She certainly looked better than when I was backstage with her after the final primaries a few weeks before.

The venue back then was telling, a cavernous basement in a public building in lower Manhattan. The lack of light and grim glares from campaign staff added to the sense of foreboding doom. The numbers would not lie and Hillary was crashing to defeat despite winning most of the delegates in the late states. She looked pale and tired, sniffling from a cold and strangely vulnerable. Her rhetoric was still upbeat, her husband was still plunging into the crowds with reckless abandon and shaking hands, but the Fat Lady was busy warbling off stage.

Now, in Washington's Mayflower, she was looking more composed, but I recalled sitting in this very hotel about a year earlier and hearing such an upbeat assessment of her chances that defeat was out of the question. In July 2007, about thirty of her closest supporters gathered at the Mayflower for an all-day seminar on the campaign. We were convinced that it was all over bar the shouting. Barack Obama was a new face who was highly unlikely to run, and if he did was sure to be crushed. The woman who hoped to be the future leader of America had gathered her brains trust here to work out the plan of campaign that would land her in the White House – or so we all believed. We were wrong.

We heard from all the heavyweights: Harold Ickes, Bill Clinton's old enforcer, pollster Mark Penn who assured us that the trends were completely in our favour. I remember one brief moment of doubt on looking around the room and figuring that everyone there was over fifty. But that was a fleeting thought. These were the pros who had delivered an unknown Arkansas governor to the White House on two occasions. They were hardly likely to fail with a far better known candidate, albeit his wife. On the campaign trail Hillary's victory had seemed assured until the voters actually cast their ballots.

The most upbeat assessment was by Terry McAuliffe, Hillary's chief fundraiser, who stated flatly that defeat looked out of the question. I would remember those words in the months to come as the impossible took shape.

A few months later I heard the same McAuliffe mantra. It was November 2007 and we were in Winterset, Iowa, in a little country hall deep in the heart of the Irish belt in a state where over 18 per cent of people were of Irish extraction. Nearby were the bridges of Madison County, made famous by the bestselling book by Robert James Waller and the Clint Eastwood film of the same name. Not far away was the farm field where, in October 1979, 300,000 Catholic Iowans had gathered to hear Pope John Paul speak to Middle America.

I had spoken ahead of McAuliffe to the fifty or so Iowans present and told them what an extraordinary job Hillary and Bill Clinton had done in helping bring peace to their ancestral land. They seemed charmed by the Clintons and glad to hear of their good deeds in Ireland. All the signs pointed positive. Outside the snow was falling but the promise of spring and political renewal seemed in the air. Mc Auliffe told them, as he had told so many before, that Hillary was so far ahead everywhere that it was only a matter of counting the votes.

Somehow, somewhere it went tragically wrong. I think I know where. The night after the Winterset meeting, Saturday, 11 November, we were in Des Moines at the Jefferson Jackson dinner. Hosted by the Democratic Party, it allows the candidates to speak at length to over 10,000 Democrats crammed into the local state fair hall. It is also the first major media event of the primary season. It is a beauty contest, a night when the candidates put on their rouge and try to make the maximum impression. I was seated at one of Hillary's tables with famed record producer Quincy Jones. The expectation was that she would hold her own with the mesmerizing young talent from Illinois who was threatening to pull off the huge upset.

When she spoke, Hillary was adequate. She was never the best speaker; is much better in intimate surroundings, talking quietly about the issues she cares most about, such as health care. That night her campaign had saddled her with a ludicrous refrain which had something to do with being able to stay in the kitchen to with-stand the heat. She referred back to it again and again but it came across as phony and hokey.

Obama could not have been more different. He bounced onto the stage and commenced a thirty-minute oration on how the country was being steered in the wrong direction, a speech that had his exuberant supporters cheering and clapping. His cadence and rhythm was that of the old-time preacher. His rhetoric was from the gut, reflecting the disgust and despair in America at large with the Bush years. In spite of my Hillary sympathies, I found myself gripped by him as was everybody else.

Beside me there was a sudden commotion. The Hillary people had come for Quincy Jones, escorting him to the side of the stage for an urgent photo op with Hillary. It was a clear attempt at a diversion – to showcase a prominent black supporter at a key moment for her main opponent. It didn't work, however – nothing would have – we were witnessing the birth of one of the most incredible political stories in American history.

The following day, David Gepsen of the local *Des Moines Register* called the Obama speech a defining moment. Coming from him it was like a pronouncement from the local Oracle. It felt like that too. Hillary never quite grabbed back the mantle of leadership after it.

Iowa proved to be a shocker of a magnitude that no one had predicted. Her gurus had expected about 150,000 people to vote in the Democratic caucus in Iowa and believed they had a winning majority at that level. In the event, 227,000 showed up, and as the busloads of Obama supports rolled in, the faces of the Clinton people got glummer and glummer. The final insult was when John Edwards shaded her for second place.

We felt like the Polish mounted cavalry that faced German tanks in September 1939 soon after the outbreak of the Second World War. We were that outdated and overpowered.

I spent days in New Hampshire as the campaign counted down and Hillary looked to be on the ropes from her shocking setback in Iowa. The Clinton canvassers were clearly being outgunned by the Obama machine. At every stoplight, at every town centre, the Obama message blared out and canvassers gathered to hoot and holler for their man.

Inside the Hillary headquarters, a shabby office in an anonymous office building, the mood was grim. The Iowa defeat had stunned the mandarins, setting off a cascade of finger pointing that would last to the very end of the campaign. Only the candidate herself seemed unperturbed, still resilient and confident despite what had happened.

Then Hillary pulled off a stunning upset in New Hampshire, and for a time it seemed that yet another chapter in the comeback saga of the Clinton family was about to unfold, but it was not to be.

Obama simply outorganized us. Whenever Hillary won a big state – and she won plenty – Obama would have locked up a caucus in a small state somewhere else where the Clinton Poo-bahs had neglected to organize, always keeping a critical margin ahead. It became like snakes and ladders, where we'd climb and tumble and climb again, always frustrated that he was just a few squares ahead of us.

I attended many Clinton campaign meetings and fundraisers during those fraught months. I was reminded vividly of the scene in the movie *Butch Cassidy and the Sundance Kid* when Robert Redford and Paul Newman keep wondering who is following and outsmarting them as they try to escape. Like Butch and Sundance we'd mutter, 'Who are those guys?' and promise to do better in the next stage.

The week of the Texas primary, I was at a fundraiser at the Dakota Building in Manhattan, famous as the location where, in December 1980, Beatle John Lennon was gunned down by Mark Chapman. It felt like a shooting this day too. Super Tuesday had just passed, Hillary had done well but not well enough, and now, for the first time, I could feel it in the air that her hard core supporters had lost heart. Even Hillary herself looked pale and wan and on her uppers. She knows she's lost it, I thought.

She fussed around as usual, spent time with my daughter, Alana, signing a campaign poster for her and asking her about third grade. She's a pro, I thought, one of the best ever. My heart went out to her. There was no stopping her and she was as fiery in her remarks as ever, drawing strength, as her husband always did, from the support around her and the love many there felt for her.

But the calculations had changed. There was nothing, short of an utter meltdown by Obama, that would give her victory. The game was up after Super Tuesday.

Now, a few months later, we were gathered in the ballroom of the Mayflower to pay homage to the new nominee of our party. In person, like many famous people close up, Barack looked impossibly young, hardly the face of a man ready to run the western world.

We spoke briefly. I asked him if he intended to go to Ireland. He flashed that wide grin. 'Of course. I have relatives from there,' he answered, referring to the Moneygall, County Offaly roots of his great great-grandfather, Falmuth Kearney. How soon would that be? 'I need to get elected first, but I'll definitely get over there,' he stated, flashing that high wattage mile. He turned to meet with someone else, but then turned back. 'I will definitely make it there as president,' he said. I could almost feel Hillary wince.

On Tuesday, 4 November 2008, I stood on 125th street in Harlem, surrounded by African Americans and giant screens as one of the most extraordinary days in American history unfolded. I interviewed Shirley Waller, a seventy-year-old woman from South Carolina who had moved to Harlem from the Deep South years before. She was the great grand-daughter of a slave and had never thought this day would come. 'I thank God I lived to see it.'

But there was still fear until the Pennsylvania result was announced – fear that somehow, some way the election would be stolen from them. The cheer that went up when the Keystone State went in the Obama column was an electric moment, as it signified certain victory. A black man was going to be president of the United States. Harlem rejoiced and it was a rare moment to share with them.

America had done it. Putting aside all the fear and negativity of the Bush years, the voters had reinvented their country and indeed the world. From Africa to Asia never again would the world look the same, with a man of colour leading the most powerful country in it.

On 20 January 2009 I stood with about a million and a half others in Washington DC as Obama was inaugurated. It was Mardi Gras and Super Bowl days all mixed up together. When Obama accepted the oath of office, a noise like rolling thunder spilled out across the stage and down through an audience that stretched as far as the eye could see. It was the sound of sheer exultation.

A few moments before, a helicopter had roared overhead, bearing the former president George Bush away to exile in Texas. The crowd began singing spontaneously, 'Na Na Na Na, Hey Hey Hey, Goodbye'. Thus in such absurd moments are political dynasties ended.

A few weeks earlier, Obama had shown his political smarts by appointing Hillary as Secretary of State. Declan Kelly, a Tipperary-born New York businessman, hosted a small brunch in her honour. He would later be named her economic envoy to Northern Ireland – an inspired choice, I thought, as he cared deeply about his home island and the issues it confronted in getting the peace process completed.

Over eggs and bacon in his Tribeca loft, Hillary held forth on the world as she saw it. She made clear that what she had experienced in Ireland would help shape her vision of the world. She spoke about the importance of special envoys such as George Mitchell to help mediate conflicts when heads of governments cannot do so. She spoke of her Irish experience of talking to previously untouchables on both sides. 'We make peace with our enemies, not our friends,' she remarked when I asked what the overwhelming lesson of the Irish peace process was for her.

That sounded right. I felt glad I had been able to help her and Bill to discover that. It had been a long journey for me.

Chapter 3

THE WISDOM OF BILL

The Clinton residence in Chappaqua, New York, a town of about 10,000 residents some thirty miles north of Manhattan, is in a cul de sac named Old House Lane. The neighbours are far closer than you might expect for the residence of a former President and First Lady of the United States. They moved in on 6 January 2000, just before Bill left the White House and Hillary took over as US senator for New York from Daniel Patrick Moynihan.

It is a beautiful old white clapboard house situated on a few acres, ironically not far from the world headquarters of the now bankrupt *Readers Digest* empire, one of the most influential right wing publications in its heyday.

On this cool autumn evening in September 2002 it was finally action time for the 2008 Hillary for President campaign. Of course it wasn't billed as such, just as a party for close friends. We were all part of a group cloyingly known as 'Hill's Angels', essentially the core group tasked originally with winning her US senate seat and eventually the White House. No one would have described it as such that night, and her presidential run was many years away, but, equally, no one was under any illusions.

'Will Hillary run for president? Does a bear shit in the woods?' as one close Clinton aide said to me pungently.

A number of us had gathered at the sprawling residence where a marquee had been set up to accommodate the attendance. Hillary greeted everyone personally, remembering spouses and kids' names in that effortless way that she and Bill have mastered. She was dressed in a summer outfit and looked more relaxed than I had seen her in years. She was clearly enjoying her term in the senate and had proven herself a dedicated and talented legislator. Now came the next step.

I knew some were urging her to run in 2004, not a strategy I favoured. The events of 9/11 had made Bush into a two-term president in my opinion, and Hillary, with only two years in the senate, would face withering criticism that she was a carpetbagger who took the seat only to run for the White House.

As the evening progressed, my wife Debbie and I took a stroll through the residence. It was clear that there was a definite geographic division of labour between the couple. Bill's study, office and gym were all on the east side of the house, while Hillary's rooms were on the opposite side. His library was packed roof to ceiling with books and, incongruously, some gym equipment. I spied three Irish titles on his shelf: a book of poems by Seamus Heaney, Conor O'Clery's book, *Daring Diplomacy,* about the Clinton work on the Irish peace process, and George Mitchell's book, *Making Peace,* on the same subject.

Outside we found Bill Clinton sitting back in an easy chair, holding court with a few friends on the state of American politics. As night began to fall, we joined the inner circle and listened to perhaps the greatest pure politician of his generation. He was discussing his favourite topic – how to win the White House – and spoke of the need to listen closely for the cadence of the times. Was it a time to run on a platform of change or to run on continuity and a steady compass? If someone was running for president, they had to know the mood music – what the American people were focused on that year – and be pitch perfect, he said.

As night drew in, the circle around Clinton grew and we hung on his words. He is always worth listening to. He is the son of a father he never knew [his father died in an accident before he was born], the stepson of an abusive alcoholic, the spurned candidate who only won the Democratic nomination in 1992 because all the insiders thought that Mario Cuomo, the popular governor of New York, was a shoo in and they decided not to run. When Cuomo pulled out, Clinton spreadeagled the field.

Now he was saying that if a politician was deaf to that mood music he or she could never succeed. Amazingly, he and Hillary made that mistake, by not running on a change agenda in 2008 six years later. No one except a complete outsider, an African American senator from Illinois, would pitch that note.

It is almost forgotten now, but Hillary's support of the Iraq war was what doomed her at the start of the 2008 campaign. The necessity to stay onside on that issue with broad American public opinion was a fundamental mistake that many other politicians also made. Perhaps Hillary's coterie can be blamed for looking past the primaries to the general election and being overconfident that she would win the nomination.

But that was all in the future back in October 2002. That night, I left Chappaqua with the clear belief that Hillary would run, not in 2004, but wait until 2008, having made a calculated decision that Bush was unbeatable in 2004, an election year bound to be overshadowed by the events of 9/11.

I was looking forward to her running for the White House in 2008. I had been there from the start of her political journey and before that for Bill's first run for the White House.

Chapter 4

HOW HILLARY EARNED
HER SPURS

The call from Hillary Clinton in the autumn of 2000 could not have been more urgent. The soft money ban, in place in her senate race against Congressman Rick Lazio in New York, which had set maximum contributions at $2,500 for individuals, meant that she was almost out of funding with the crucial last few weeks in the race yet to come. Could I organise a major fundraiser, one that the president himself would attend if we could swing at least $150,000 in hard cash, she asked. I thought it over for a few seconds before responding that yes, I could do that. After putting down the phone I wondered if my enthusiasm had not over-whelmed my judgment. Getting 150 people separately to write a cheque for $1,000 was an uphill battle, particularly in a community where many held very mixed views on the Clinton White House.

Over the next few days I ransacked every filofax entry I had, and with enormous help from Steven Travers, one of my work associates, began calling around non-stop. I got some blunt refusals; others promised help but never delivered. The majority, however, hard-working Irish businessmen and women, were only too happy to oblige. Because of the Clintons' extraordinary role in the Irish peace process there was a reservoir of goodwill and commitment there that had never been truly tapped. Many of the contributors were staunch Republican party members who appreciated above all else what the Clintons had done in Ireland. I discovered that the best way to fundraise was to get a few heavy hitters who could then bring in five or ten others, who could bring in a few more, in a sort of daisy chain reaction that ensured that we reached out the length and breadth of the Irish community in New York. Thus several leaders in the Irish community signed on as co-chairs. Soon the total began mounting, until I fully used up the favour bank I had built up over many years in New York. We passed the $100,000 mark and headed confidently for the magic $150,000. The Clinton staffers were obviously astonished. At the end of a long drawn out political campaign – the most expensive senate race in history – they thought they had tapped every conceivable donor and ethnic group, but here were the Irish, delivering.

On the night itself, some 200 or so of us packed the lobby and bar area of Fitzpatrick's Hotel in midtown Manhattan. It was a crush, as it always is at Clinton functions, with everyone determined to get close enough to get a photograph with the world's most famous couple. As MC and chief organiser I was run off my feet trying to cater to every big contributor. Worse, of course, the Clintons were late, as they always are, and Hillary arrived before Bill, throwing our programme into chaos. As always, Hillary was cool and calm despite the crush of bodies. One of the secrets often missed about the Clintons is how much they actually enjoy the flesh pressing part of the political game. Whereas most people would recoil from another sweaty room and hordes of excited devotees trying to grasp their hand, I have seen both Clintons thrive on it on many occasions.

When she began her senate race, Hillary was more standoffish, but by the end she was almost a match for her husband, one of the most electric personalities ever to light up a room. As First Lady, Hillary had often seemed aloof, and many of her supporters questioned whether the rough and tumble of political life as a candidate would suit her. They need not have worried. Hillary was also very comfortable with the press, something not generally realised because of all the scrutiny she has undergone.

Once, when hosting her at a St Patrick's Day event in 2000, there were throngs of media waiting to interrogate her upstairs in O'Neill's restaurant. A small group of us huddled together downstairs to prepare her for possible questions. Midway through my briefing on Irish issues I realised she was actually looking forward to the grilling, to giving as good as she got and walking the tightrope of unscripted media appearances, which fewer and fewer politicians do. She strode upstairs almost eagerly, the light of battle in her eye, ready to face the klieg lights and the assembled horde.

On this night in October 2000, when I introduced Hillary I talked humorously, I hope, about the 'Irish' senate seat she was running for, one held by Daniel Patrick Moynihan, Kevin Keating, William Buckley and many other Irish Americans, going back decades. Even though she wasn't directly Irish, I said, we were going to accept her as one of our own, and no Italian like Lazio was going to take the 'Irish' seat. She enjoyed that and she launched into a spirited outline of all she and her husband had done for the Irish peace process. She was interrupted several times by tumultuous applause. After her remarks, Hillary went upstairs to a holding room to await her husband who had been delayed. I sat out in the front bar area where he was going to make his entrance, with some secret service people and John Fitzpatrick, a close personal friend and owner of the hotel and a man who had devoted enormous time and energy to the Clinton cause over the years.

Hillary joined us and we stood chatting for over ten minutes while waiting for the president to arrive. When he did, it was his usual bear-hugging, backslapping entrance, striding into the cordoned-off room and immediately becoming the centre of gravity. He posed for pictures with the bartender, with John Fitzpatrick and me. Then he and Hillary huddled together for a few moments, within earshot. Seeing them together for any extended period of time you cannot but be struck by the easy body language. Numerous books have been written, and indeed an entire industry has grown up, speculating on their relationship. Having seen them close up and so easy with each other on innumerable occasions, the answer seems obvious to me. Despite all the difficulties and trials of the past decade, they remain in love and indeed infatuated with each other.

She visibly relaxes in his company. He often plays the jokester, anxious to put her at her ease. He talks, she listens. He leans in, forming almost a protective barrier around her. She can be remote, tightlipped and distant in certain situations, but never around him. There have obviously been tradeoffs, as there are in most relationships, but they have stayed together for over thirty-five years, far longer than the relationships of many of their chief critics who espouse 'family values'. On this evening he was advising her about an aspect of her campaign for senator. He has a computer-like facility to remember even the most arcane aspects of any political race and he was telling her the percentage of the vote he thought she needed to get in several upstate counties. 'Governor Pataki got 71 per cent there in his last election' he told her, referring to some remote New

York state region, 'I think you can get over 50 percent'.

When he was in Dublin in 1995, in Cassidy's bar, he regaled Congressman Tom Manton and me with the figures from almost every precinct in Queens from the 1992 presidential election. When he had finished and moved on, Manton, the Queens' Democratic leader and an old-style boss, turned to me and said, 'He knows more about votes in Queens than I do'.

When we entered the main lobby from our private meeting in the bar, you had the immediate sense of a room listing to one side, as the crush to meet the president became an unruly scene. Perfectly poised businessmen and women who were calmly sipping cocktails and munching on hors d'oeuvres, suddenly dropped all pretence of sophistication and rushed to meet and greet Clinton. With great difficulty we established a receiving line and I stood beside the Clintons to ensure that everyone they met was properly introduced. It is always astonishing to watch people's behaviour in Bill Clinton's presence. 'Clutchers' is the secret service name for those who just won't let go, and there were quite a few in our crowd. One woman in particular did everything but strip in front of him, rubbing her breasts against him and clutching on to his hand until I gently disengaged it. I saw Hillary signalling to me when another woman engaged her and her husband in a discussion about her dreams, which included the nugget that she dreamt about Bill every night. These people apart, the Clintons seemed to genuinely enjoy the warmth of the welcome. Bill, as one aide said, is addicted to 'junk love' – the extraordinary reaction he gets from crowds. This evening he was a trifle weary by the end of the handshaking, however, and asked me in a humorous aside if I was going out into the street to bring people in to meet him.

After his brief speech I escorted him back through the curtain into the bar area where we stopped for a few moments and chatted about the North. As usual, he listened intently. His ability to soak up knowledge on a myriad of complex issues is perhaps his greatest political talent. I knew this was the last time I would see him as president and I thanked him for all he had done to bring peace to my country, the first president who ever cared enough about it. As we walked to the door he suddenly put his arm on my shoulders, looked me in the eye and said, 'We did some great work together, didn't we?' I couldn't think of a better tribute than that to my time in America. I had come a long way too.

Chapter 5

MY FATHER'S DREAM

We walked along the road to the beach. He gripped my hand in that urgent way reserved for fathers walking with their sons, not as comfortable or steady as my mother's. He was at home here. It was his place: West Kerry with its soaring mountains and mutinous sea crashing endlessly against the rugged shoreline. His family had been here for several generations and his nephew still farmed the lumpy land just a few miles from the beach. He knew every field, every yard of the old homestead. He even knew the ghosts. He told me he thought they walked beside him, those solemn spectres of family past. I know he talked to them in Irish, the native language still spoken in this remote part of Ireland. He missed them all, he told me, and more than ever now that he was bringing their grandchildren down to this most westerly part of Ireland.

Years later I would go back and find out who he was communing with.

❦

When the 1911 Irish census first came on line it covered only four counties: Antrim, Dublin, Down and Kerry. Luckily, the O'Dowd old homestead in the townland of Kilcooley, about seven miles from Dingle, was included. My brother Fergus called me excitedly from Ireland and referred me to the Kilcooley parish records from 1911 – and there, at last, was my father's family.

It was an extraordinary moment to reach out and touch the souls who came before me and made me what I am today. Some names I knew, others I never would. They were there under the heading: 'Residents of House No. 8, Kilcooley, Kerry'. My great-grandfather, Edward Dowd (they didn't use the 'O' back then) was the family patriarch in 1911. He was seventy-two years old and married with four children.

He signed his census form with an X, which meant he was not literate, a fact the census taker duly noted. He had been born just a few years before the famine in 1839 and had gone through it. Edward was a farmer, and he and wife Mary, 69, had married in 1861 and raised four kids there in their two-room house and small farm. Now, in 1911, they shared the two-room house with thirteen others – an incredible number of people, but a fair indication of the awful economic times.

There was Michael, my grandfather, and his wife, Catherine Kennedy, from a nearby townland. They were aged 45 and 38 respectively when the census was taken on the night of 2 April 1911. I remember my grandmother dimly, my grandfather not at all. They had nine children at that point and the census taker noted that ten had been born but one did not survive – something none of my family today ever knew. There was Mary who went to Detroit, Jack who followed her there, Michael, who would eventually inherit the farm, Ellen, who became a nun in Savannah, Georgia, then Patrick, who became a priest in the black hills of South Dakota; there too was Donal, my father, five years old on 2 April 1911, who later became a schoolteacher.

Underneath his name were those of Edward, who went to London, and Thomas who became a Christian Brother. Not yet born were Dennis, who also became a Christian Brother, Brid who came to New York, and Matt who became a Christian Brother and died tragically young. Also living in the house at the time were two of my grandfather's brothers.

Everyone was listed as farmer or scholar, except for my grandfather's brother, who was listed as a fisherman. Everyone except Edward was literate, but only in the Irish language. It seemed from the census that there were more people living in my great-grandfather's house than in any other home in the parish. A family called the O'Connors had a six-room house, which must have made them the envy of the Dowds and everyone else locally.

What amazed me too was the fact that, almost a hundred years later, the same families still occupy the village. Next door, as they were in 1911, are the Hurleys and the Sheas. The old homestead is now farmed by my cousin Padraig. We know from Griffiths' Valuations, an 1852 survey of land prices in West Kerry, that Michael and Mary Dowd were living in Kilcooley back then, though there is no further information on them. There is a wonderful timelessness to all this, the sense that the rhythms of life in an isolated part of rural Ireland pass down from generation to generation. I felt that a chapter on a previous life of my father's family had suddenly been opened up and the history suddenly come to life.

That was all in the future, of course. On this day when I was young, my father and I reached the beach and walked to the end of the pier. We gazed out at the vast expanse of water and the headland in the distance. The clouds were settling in over Mount Eagle, a harbinger of rain to come. A distant roll of thunder echoed across the bay. A storm was coming. Other children were there with their parents, shouting and laughing. A little boy ran past, pursued by his father as they raced to their car to beat the storm. I realised for the first time that mine was older than most of the fathers and that he would find it hard to run so fast. It didn't bother me. He didn't seem to mind the rain as it fell and the sky darkened. His eyes were fixed on the wide horizon, staring far out to sea, past the crashing waves. 'What is out there, Dad?' I asked him. He looked at me, smiling. 'America,' he said. 'That's the next parish.' It was the first time I had ever heard of the place.

Chapter 6

CALIFORNIA HERE I COME

There's a stretch of wilderness, like a no-man's-land, between Wyoming and Salt Lake City, where what seems like thousands of miles of hard sand and rock undulate on either side of the highway. On a clear summer's night in 1978, with a full moon reflecting eerily on the lunar-like landscape, it was like nothing I had ever seen. Inside the Greyhound bus speeding me across this vista I was conscious of a great stirring.

I was twenty-five years old and truly on my own for the first time. Behind me lay the East Coast and the city of Chicago, where I had spent the past six months. Ahead lay the Western shores, first Nevada and beyond that California – my final destination. There is a moment, as Solzhenitsyn has remarked, that your life leads up to and everything after leads away from forever. This was mine. Perhaps it had been the lights of Cheyenne reflecting in the rear view mirror of the bus and that lonely, indescribable feeling as I faced into the night and the unknown. Maybe it was the sheer enormity of the land we now travelled through that brought about the dawning realisation that nothing again would ever be the same. Nor would it be.

Back in Chicago, just two hours after I had left, a telegram arrived informing me of my father's heart attack back home in Ireland. If I had stayed, or even been delayed by a day, I would have immediately rushed home to be with him. The attack was not fatal, but a later one soon after would kill him. If I had returned from Chicago I would have been there when he died from the second attack. I would have settled down in Ireland and become the schoolteacher he so desperately wanted me to be. I would have figured, fatalistically, that my life had taken that turn for a reason and would have just allowed myself to be carried along in the familiar flow of family, a decent job and lots of friends. It was not to be, because of a two-hour time lag.

Strangely, my father had said goodbye to me on the phone just the week before, calling me up out of the blue to chat about America, a land he had never seen but which lived vividly in his imagination. He had given me my love of it, filling my childish head full of tales of westerns and Zane Grey novels where the heroes always looked cool and clean. Cowboy films were one of his few relaxations away from his seven children, and he replayed many of the scenes to me from memory. I loved the old movies too; titles like *The Man from Laramie* and *Shane* were part of my boyhood mythology. Finally I was living the dream I had had since I was a kid, of travelling to the American West. Indeed, since I was a child all of America had taken a grip on my imagination. I loved Superman comics and the visits home by my uncle, a priest in South Dakota. I was enchanted when he talked about the endless plains and the vast prairies where one could drive for a full day and never meet anyone, and the crashing thunderstorms and bolt lightning that lit up the night sky like day.

The life I lived in Ireland, solidly middle class, one of seven children of my father, a schoolteacher from Kerry, and my mother, a housewife from Clare, seemed sadly unoriginal by comparison. Because he was quite deaf at that stage, communication was difficult with my father during our final phone call, but I told him what

I could about how well I was doing, the thing each parent wants to hear, despite the reality of my circumstances. I would always be glad of that last awkward goodbye.

Now I would never see him again and the telegram would pursue me across the United States, arriving ten days later when I was settled in California. As he lay ill and on his final journey I was on the Greyhound bus contemplating a rebirth, a new life in a land where I knew no one, having cut all the ties to Chicago and home. I had never felt happier in my life. I knew nothing of his illness, intent on my American odyssey.

Years later, my mother told me that when he heard I planned to move to San Francisco from Chicago, he had studied maps of America from his hospital bed and plotted my course from Chicago to San Francisco with the excitement of a wagon train scout planning a new route. Perhaps he was with me on this trip, a ghostly presence out beyond the flatlands. Indeed, during a fitful sleep on the Greyhound bus I dreamt vividly of him that night. I even jotted down a note about it when I awoke. In the dream I pictured him as I saw him on one of the last occasions in the Franciscan Church in Drogheda, my home town, half way up the aisle, a short, stocky man with his black cap for once in his pocket. He was kneeling, as he always did, yet in his own world, too deaf to hear the prayers, too proud to admit it to anyone but his family. In the dream he was reading from his old Irish language missal, the one with the ornate symbols and exotic Irish phrases. He caressed it often, as though it was one of his children. The litany of the saints always sounded much more intriguing in the Irish language, the fine strong words tripping off his tongue; he had a beautiful lilt when he spoke the language. I would remember that dream forever. Ever after, on hearing the booming opening lines of his favourite prayer in

English: 'Hail Holy Queen, Mother of Mercy, Hail our life, our sweetness and our hope', it would take me back to that moment.

Sometimes he would meet his friend, Stephen Ryan, like him an Irish speaker, and they would drive in Ryan's old Fiat to the seaside, usually to Mornington, a sleepy little village just four miles from town. There the Irish Sea washed in, far calmer than the bold Atlantic on the other side of the country, and the hungry seagulls perched on top of the ruins of an old abbey. Cars carrying courting couples parked near the water and waited for the onset of nightfall. From across the fields you could often hear the tolling of the Mornington church bell, its rich peal echoing over the strand. On clear days my father and Ryan could look across the bay and see Ireland's Eye, the little island perched off the Irish coast, and further on the shimmering lights of North Dublin, the gateway to the big city. Sometimes they drove in that direction, but they never actually reached it. They were two country men, not really at home in the big cities. Ryan was a travelling salesman and had spent a lifetime traversing the highways and byways of Ireland and he knew every twist and turn. My father had travelled little, never learning to drive.

Once I was lucky enough to accompany them to Mornington. We drove out on a harsh night with rain spitting against the windows of the tiny car. I sat in the back, wedged behind the front seats. I was eleven or twelve at the time, fast coming into maturity. They spent the entire time talking about how scandalised they were at the appearance in Dublin of American film star and sex symbol Jayne Mansfield. A sex symbol in Ireland! I couldn't wait to read about her and dreamt about seeing her in the flesh.

The sins of the flesh, of course, were non-existent in Ireland at the time, or so we were led to believe. A generation later it would all come spilling out about paedophile priests, the horrific abuse in some orphanages and the dreadful acts committed on some single mothers who were forced to give up their children and live in total servitude. Back in the Ireland of the 1960s, grim, brooding and bitter, you didn't try and stand up or stand out, you just conformed, even as a kid. You knew better than to question your elders and betters. A fundamentalist mindset reigned. 'Who made the world?' 'God made the world.' No room for doubt there.

That all seemed far behind me now. Now I was in Jayne Mansfield's country: rich, voluptuous, different. The bus sped on. From time to time we pulled off the highway into some unnamed or unremembered town, stopped briefly to discharge or take on a passenger. The night sky was star spangled all the way to the horizon, the moon was full and the only sound apart from the hum of the bus was a soughing wind when you opened the windows to breathe in the perfect air. From the back of the bus wafted the acrid smell of a marijuana joint, and later some muffled giggling. Two black guys I had befriended at the Cheyenne stop were doing the smoking. When I invited them into the bar near the bus stop they politely declined. Once inside, I knew why. Everyone there was white and they would hardly have been welcome.

Inside the bar I got into conversation with two cowboys seated at the counter. One told me he thought Ireland was somewhere off Africa. The other inquired, for some reason, about exporting cars to Ireland. I found it all exotic and exciting. Back on the bus after hours of crossing the flat terrain, Salt Lake City finally loomed in the distance, home of the Mormons, and not much else that I knew about it. As we traversed the downtown streets it seemed like a ghost town, with no one except occasional cops and a bum or two in sight. The Greyhound bus terminal was in a seedy part of town, as they invariably are, and the brightly lit waiting room was the only oasis in what seemed a dark and unfriendly neighbourhood. This was my terminus too, the place where I would pick up another bus to California. Within an hour I would have to choose between a bus to San Francisco or Los Angeles, a decision that would alter the course of my life forever.

In retrospect, my decision was obvious, but at the time it hardly seemed so clear cut. I was expecting this to be the definitive journey of my life, not merely another passage to some unknown place. San Francisco had been part of my imagination since the Scott McKenzie song of that name strummed its way into my head several years before. As a student in Dublin, damp and dreary nights in cold apartments were often whiled away dreaming of California. Since I was a child it had fired my imagination, why I will never know, yet it had been a constant urge to go there. Now I was finally on the way.

Los Angeles was also an option because a friend of a friend in Chicago had invited me to go there and work with him. It was not a city that had ever inspired me, however, but the prospect of a definite job and a place to stay after this exhausting trek across country was inviting. My ticket terminated in Salt Lake and as I waited in line to buy passage to my next destination I felt an eerie calm about the decision I was about to make.

San Francisco seemed an antidote to life in narrow, constricted Ireland, a place where they wore flowers in their hair and nobody cared where you were from or where you were going and where there seemed a sense of youthful idealism and a real meaning to life. There was also a name I had of someone in San Francisco, one Martin Mulkerrins, a brother of a good friend of mine in Chicago. I

41

didn't know his address or phone number, merely the name of the tavern called 'The Abbey' that he hung out in. It was better than nothing, and besides, it was an improvement over Los Angeles for which I felt no tug at my soul. San Francisco it would be. After a two-hour wait, the bus finally pulled out of the station as dawn was breaking. I settled back in my old seat, conscious that the two young black men had disembarked and that I knew not a living soul from here to California. I suddenly loved that feeling. Soon we drove through the Salt Lake itself, resplendent in the dawn light, how I imagined the Dead Sea would look in a scene from biblical times. It was easy to see why a man would put down camp and establish his church here under what one writer later called the 'Banner of Heaven'.

As we went further west the terrain had begun to change. The flat monotony of Iowa, Idaho, Nebraska and the plains states were behind us, and first the foothills and then the sheer stark ridges of the Sierra Nevada loomed in front of us. What a bountiful land, I thought, looking at the lakes, streams, rivers, mountains and forests that had begun to dot the landscape in the morning light. I could picture the old pioneers, so many of them Irish, coming across this land after the exhausting trek across the plains and imagining they had reached Nirvana. A hundred years or so later, that's how it looked to me as well. In Ireland, from the tip of one end to the extreme at the other, the island is no more than 350 miles long. I would travel that distance in a single day now and still make no dent on the never-ending land-scape which stretched out in front of me.

The notion of following the horizon without falling into the ocean I found a very powerful one. Sometimes I felt miscast in this century, much preferring to have tackled these same hills and mountains as part of a pioneering expedition. In a strange way, as I watched the landscape slip by, I felt I was back to where I had never actually been. If there was such a thing as a previous life I believed I must have spent part of it here in the American West. Our first stop on the bus was Reno, an isolated bluff of a town lying at Nevada's northern edge. The opening lines of the old song 'Don't Go Down to Reno'... 'In Reno town for a few dollars down' played in my head as I made my way to the casino near the bus station. It was early morning and I was weary. There was just enough time to lose some money on the gaming machine before the last leg of the journey to San Francisco commenced.

Somewhere between Reno and San Francisco, a group of motor-cyclists began buzzing the bus, first three in front and three behind, then all six riding perilously close together just a few bumpers' space from the bus itself. Though the driver tooted his horn and hollered, they were obviously having great fun. Finally the leader of the pack, a heavyset, bearded guy, stood up straight in his saddle while his female pillion passenger pulled his jeans down to reveal his butt cheeks to the startled bus passengers. Some of us laughed, others looked away in disgust. As a cheeky welcome to California, it took some beating.

It was late evening when we reached the San Francisco Greyhound bus station. By now I was sufficiently exhausted to have slept the last hour of the journey or so but I woke up disoriented, having dreamt that I was back in Ireland playing football. Instead, here I was, inside a station in a seedy part of the Mission district with a backpack and about $200 dollars in cash. The effect was like a cold shower, the grand dreams and designations of the bus trip giving way to a scary reality. The old saying that it is sometimes better to travel than to arrive crossed my mind. Now it would be a matter of taking care of basics such as food, work and accommodation.

A good-looking young couple accosted me as I walked towards the station entrance. They were members of a commune, they explained, and I was welcome to join them if I so wished. The woman was blonde and California looking, with glasses perched on her forehead, the man clean and well dressed and very polite. 'Do you need a place to stay or some food?' they asked. It was a California cliché come alive for me. Years later I figured they were probably Moonies. Luckily, after briefly entertaining their offer, I declined.

Once outside, I asked directions to the Abbey Tavern on 5th and Geary, and was directed to a nearby bus stop. Having eventually figured out how to pay the fare, I found myself on a bus travelling up Geary Boulevard with Ocean Beach as its final destination, a route that would soon become very familiar to me. San Francisco was beautiful. The moonlight played off the Victorian mansions, their colours a pale kaleidoscope of blues, yellows and pinks, all the different colours giving off a warm glow. The hills were majestic and magnificent as the bus clambered up each one en route to the Richmond District. The bus seemed to pause as if to catch its breath before the top of each hill and the next traffic light. In the distance I could see the twinkling lights of San Francisco Bay and the looming mansions of Nob Hill that the very rich called home. This was like nowhere I had ever been before, a city yes, but a magical place too, where the very air seemed full of possibilities and a young man's imagination would find room to breathe. I was well pleased with myself.

The Abbey was a hive of activity when I stepped inside. A large pool table in a side room was a central gathering point, while the bar itself was circular in shape and extended fully around the room. On the wall were faded photos and mementos of Ireland. In one of them a donkey ambled happily down a country road, in another an old Guinness ad: a man balancing a horse and cart over his head after getting the energy from drinking a pint of the black stuff. The place had a somewhat rundown feel, which added somehow to its attraction. I learnt later that during the day it was man's bar, a hard-drinking oasis in a city where alcohol was becoming decidedly uncool. Late at night, however, the big old bar would fill up with wives and girlfriends and single girls intent on meeting a lonely Irishman. Then the atmosphere changed.

I pulled up a stool to the bar and eyed the clientele. Who to ask here about Martin Mulkerrins? I immediately saw my target; amid the blond and bleached California looks was a man with a map of Ireland face, dressed for all the world like he was ready for a night out in a West of Ireland ballroom around 1955. I strolled over and tapped him on the shoulder.

'Hello, I'm just off the bus from back east and I'm looking for Martin Mulkerrins,' I announced.

'Martin?' he said, hardly skipping a beat. 'He was here about a half hour ago but he left. You'll probably find him at the Blarney Stone – it's on twenty-second and Geary.' He paused for a moment, no doubt taking in my long hair, straggly beard and generally unkempt appearance. 'Where are you from yourself?' 'Tipperary,' I answered, the place where I was born before our family moved to Drogheda in County Louth when I was ten, knowing it was a safe enough answer and glad I didn't have to say 'Dublin'. If I had, there would have been an immediate mistrust. 'Jackeens' were generally considered too clever by half by other emigrants.

'Oh, right so. Well, I'm from Mayo. Will you have a drink?' he offered.We sat and drank a beer and then he ordered two shots, which I had, of course, to reciprocate. Already I could feel the $200 beginning to seep away, not to mention a warm buzz filling my head. 'This is a good town,' he told me, having introduced himself as Pat Curran. 'Plenty of work for them that want it. Good weather all year round. Constructions indoors, outdoors, no winter season like Chicago and back east. If you can play Gaelic football you'll get along fine.'

The last point was one I knew already. For generations, young Irish-men like myself had made their way to America to play Gaelic games. If you had no relatives in the country it was about the best way to get your start. The teams, if you were very good, paid your fare out and got you work. If you were even a little above average they could ensure that you got the all important 'start' or first job in construction. 'Any chance of the start?' was a common refrain. Playing football was also a wonderful way to make friends, to bed down with your own kind. Years later, I often heard people remark scathingly that the young Irish wanted to stick with their own, making it some kind of criticism of them. What else would you do straight off the plane and in a strange land? There would be lots of time to find out about the great American culture later on. Thus, skill at Ireland's national game, played fervently by exiles all over America, was the equivalent of a ticket to travel and to work.

I wasn't the greatest player around, but had the advantage of being relatively new from Ireland at a time when not many were coming over. In San Francisco that was even more the case. If five or six journeymen with football skills arrived every summer that would be it. I was part of this year's crop. I knew that Martin Mulkerrins was tied in with one of the San Francisco teams, so that could be my ticket to a job and putting a roof over my head. I had made the mistake back in Chicago of aligning myself with one of the poorest teams who could provide very little in the way of job opportunities or accommodation. I was not about to make that same mistake here. After another round of drinks I said goodbye to my new-found friend and stepped outside the Abbey bar. I gazed up for a long time at the California sky and thought of all the times in my dreams I had come to this place and time. Now I had actually arrived. It was time to get started on my new life.

Chapter 7

SAN FRANCISCO DREAMING

The Irish neighbourhoods in San Francisco – the Sunset and the Richmond – were adjacent to each other, separated at their furthest points by Golden Gate Park. Each was bordered by the ocean, spectacularly so. Ocean Beach is one of the most beautiful urban stretches of strand in the world, with the Pacific breakers reaching shore within a taxi ride of downtown San Francisco. Each neighbourhood was home to a polyglot of constantly changing cultures, but a strong Irish presence remained despite the shifting cultural sands around them.

Here it was that generations of Irish emigrants made their living, by my time mostly by constructing what came to be mockingly called 'Micktorians' – basic two-family apartments about as far removed from the glorious Victorian mansions as Los Angeles is from San Francisco. The Irish would make no apologies for that. Most of the emigrants in the 1970s and before had left hopeless lives on small farms on the western seaboard. Not for them the endless grind of their fathers' lives, making enough on the Fair Day to keep going for another few months. They got out, and the luckiest of them came to California. Building dreary apartments in California wasn't a bad option, given the alternatives, and the weather was surely a lot better.

Many had stopped off in Alaska first, lured by the work on the giant oil pipeline there. References to places like Prudhoe Bay and Fairbanks were as common as talking about Dublin or Cork in many Irish circles. 'When it's Springtime in Alaska', a country and western song, was on as many jukeboxes in Irish bars as any Irish song. Those who went to Alaska were inevitably marked by the experience. The money was great, of course, and many arrived in San Francisco with a life's fortune. But the conditions were cruel, sometimes nineteen-hour days, and the long and interminable stretches of boredom and loneliness in the far north affected some men for the rest of their lives. Some could not cope with what San Francisco offered after they left the wilderness, and drank, drugged and whored themselves into a kind of permanent stupor. Occasionally you would see one of these stumblebums falling around the place as the bars closed. Other times they would show up at the Gaelic games, standing away on their own, lonely figures shunned by many, or, sadly, made fun of by others.

The majority, however, used their cash wisely and started construction businesses. Many were the same age as me, twenty-five when I arrived in California, but were already well on their way to millions in their mid-twenties. I had no such background, of course, and was barely passable as a construction worker, something I had learned to my cost in Chicago. Having two left hands was part of the problem, but a pronounced fear of heights when balancing on a scaffold or a forty-foot ladder didn't help either. Later I would learn that there was something about California that crept into the soul of Irish men there, made them more congenial, less eager to judge or hurl the bitter word like so many of their countrymen back east. But when I arrived I was intent only on finding work and a place to live. That was proving difficult to do that first night.

I arrived at the Blarney Stone to discover that Martin Mulkerrins had just left, and I felt suddenly like I was chasing a ghost. A few more beers gave me the courage to talk to some other Irish men at the bar. They felt certain that Martin would be at the dance that night in the nearby church hall, hosted by the Sean MacDermott's football team. I could surely find him there. I walked out into the night air which had now turned decidedly chilly and damp. Unknown to me, I was experiencing the famed San Francisco fog for the first time. I had my bag and about $150 in cash. I had to make a connection at the dance. Finding the church hall was no easy matter. The church itself, an old Spanish style adobe building, was easily located, but the hall was tucked away at the back. I could hear the sound of the Irish music, but could not find an entrance. Finally, in desperation, I clambered over a wire fence and crossed what seemed like a school playground, in the direction of where the music was coming from. Eventually I arrived at a church door and a sign which read 'Parish Hall'. Once inside, I discovered I could have been back in any parish hall in Ireland.

The band, as the posters advertised, was from Boston: John Connors and the Lightning Express – a rare treat for the San Francisco Irish. They belonged in a ballroom in Mayo, not here in this city by the bay, 6,000 miles from there. They were blasting out the old country numbers to a packed hall and it took me some time to negotiate the heaving and swaying mass to get to the bar. A giant of a man, who looked to be in his early thirties, with thick curly hair, stood at the bar nursing a Budweiser. Over the din of the music I shouted that I was looking for Martin Mulkerrins. He took a long look at me and said in Irish, '*Tá tú ag caint leis.*' (You're talking to him.) I breathed a sigh of relief. At long last, a stroke of luck. I mentioned his brother in Chicago and said that he had told me to look him up.

'I know. I was looking for you too. Have a beer. You're staying with me tonight.' No sweeter words had ever been uttered to me. Bushed after the long journey and feeling the light-headed effects of too much beer, I was only too anxious to find a bed to lie down. Martin, however, was going to enjoy the dance for a while more. We stayed at the bar sipping our beer and I learnt quickly that he was a man of few words and one of the most relaxed human beings you could ever be around. Nothing bothered him. He fitted right into San Francisco, where laid back was a way of life.

The women were beautiful, and tired as I was, I could not but admire that golden California look that so many sported. Many of the dancers seemed to know the Irish dances and soon the floor was a whirling dervish of couples turning and dancing in different direction. It was a captivating moment. Here it seemed every person in the room was out for the 'Siege of Ennis' or the 'Walls of Limerick', swirling around the floor with great abandon. A pretty young girl grasped my hand to partner her in one of the waltzes. I couldn't believe my luck that a woman had asked me to dance. As we stumbled around the floor she told me she was a schoolteacher and a native San Franciscan whose father was from Ireland. She seemed to know more about 'the old country' than I did and reeled off a list of places she had stayed on vacations over there. I hardly got a word in edgeways. We danced a few more sets and she gave me her phone number; such a display of forwardness would have been unheard of for an Irish woman back home. I liked her but was simply too tired to even think about following up.

At around two o'clock that morning, Martin had enough and we went outside where he slung my canvas bag into the back seat of his car and we set off for his home, a modest two-bedroom apartment in the Richmond district, just a stone's throw from the ocean.The address was 1418 La Playa, an anonymous apartment building, but I would not have been happier to see the Waldorf Astoria.

I met his roommate, a fellow Connemara man, Tom MacDonagh, who, amazingly, I knew from Chicago where he had been a roommate of a friend of mine. The omens were good. I had just enough energy to shake hands and exchange pleasantries before falling dead asleep on a mattress on the floor. I had made it to California and had a roof over my head. Things hadn't started off too badly, unlike when I had first moved from Ireland to Chicago.

Chapter 8

THE CITY OF BROAD SHOULDERS

'In the city of Chicago
As the evening shadows fall
There are people dreaming
Of the Hills of Donegal'

W hen I landed in Chicago in the summer of 1978 I had struggled mightily to put a basic life together. It started when I joined the wrong Irish football team – St Mel's – the weakest of the Chicago area sides. That meant no easy job in construction or an apartment share. But St Mel's had paid my flight out so I was beholden to them. At the time I knew no difference between the teams, so I was very happy to get the subsidised trip. That morning I had bid goodbye to Ireland and to my parents, my father, as it turned out, for the last time. At my version of an American wake the night before I had got thoroughly drunk with my best friend Eddie Holt and confided in him my desire to leave for America for good. 'I'm making the break,' I told Eddie as we sipped our beers. 'I'm like a fish out of water over here, I need something else.'

'Be careful what you wish for,' he responded. 'If America doesn't work out, you might be forced to come back here with your tail between your legs. Now that might prove very awkward.' He was right of course, yet I didn't care. That night we took our usual late night walk around town, out to the furthest streetlight on the road towards the town of Navan. It was raining, a dull drumbeat that splattered off the slatternly roofs of the small cottages we passed on our way. I wouldn't miss this, I thought, not at all. Well after midnight we went back to his house to drink a few beers while his parents slept upstairs. I felt oddly exhilarated as if the witching hour had come for me and a journey long contemplated was about to begin.

I had little choice but to leave. School teaching, I had discovered, was not for me. I lacked both the patience and the temperament for a job that I had always aspired to. A year in an inner city Dublin school, barely holding an unruly class in check, had convinced me of my mistake in my first career choice. Some of the other teachers I knew held their classes together by sheer fear and meted out corporal punishment at will. I was unable to do that, having suffered from it too much in my own schooldays. I had the idea that I would be a different kind of teacher and that the pupils would become my friends, but I learnt all too quickly that this was a mere pipe dream which shattered on contact with reality.

It was tough to teach kids some of whom undoubtedly did not have enough to eat that morning. At the parent/teacher meetings, I quickly learnt that it was always the parents you wanted most to see about their errant kids who never showed up. All in all, a dispiriting experience and one that convinced me that I needed to look elsewhere. It had finally come to a head when I came unmercifully close to hitting one kid who had been bothering me for some time. As a Christian Brothers' boy, I had been well used to getting physically knocked around by some of the bullying brothers and lay teachers, but I didn't ever want to be part of that mindset myself. The psychology involved in teaching had changed, I realised. Whereas in my father's time it was a prestigious job with the emphasis on learning, now it was more a matter of just keeping order for successive forty-five-minute spells.

The only time I had felt good about myself in the role was teaching night classes in the Dublin suburb of Finglas, which had ferocious social problems. The area had originally been set up by relocating families from the tenements in the centre of Dublin. It was a disastrous move. Whereas they had at least a sense of community in the city centre, in Finglas they lived on soulless, sprawling estates where the only patch of green was some miserable vegetable gardens some residents tried to grow. However, because the night class pupils were adult and obviously highly motivated, I communicated much better, learnt a lot and enjoyed the experience thoroughly.

So I knew I had to move on. But to where? In Ireland at the time there were very few other options: unemployment was a booming business and the emigrant trains and planes were starting to fill up after years of relative prosperity. I had a visa allowing me to work for four months in the US. It seemed the only way out.

Chapter 9

THE LEAVETAKING

The next morning, still suffering from the effects of the booze, I staggered downstairs at 9 o'clock. Outside the skies were a gun metal grey and rain sweeping in from the west was forecast. Some things never changed. A deep sepulchral gloom hung over the household. My mother cooked her usual gargantuan breakfast – her greatest fear was always that one of her brood would go hungry. Her heart wasn't in it this morning, however. Only since becoming a parent myself do I realise how difficult it is to part from a child. I didn't really know then, but I know now that it must have broken her heart each time a member of her family took off for foreign climes.

My father was not a demonstrative man but he threw his arms around me in a rare display of emotion. Then he waited out in our back garden as I climbed the embankment to the nearby railway bridge in Drogheda, a fast short cut to the station. He watched as I walked across the railway lines spanning the river Boyne to the train station proper. Did he suspect that this was the last time he would see his son? I would never know the answer to that but my mother said he seemed more upset than was usual when one of his brood of seven went away, as was a frequent occurrence. I think of him now, as I became a smaller and smaller speck on the horizon, walking further away from him at every step. I don't know if he was thinking those dread thoughts of his own mortality, so close to his own death, but there was no question that he must have felt a deep sense of loss.

⬥

Later, my mother told me that my father plotted every yard of my journey, picking each of the cities I flew over en route to Chicago, living the trip he had never taken but had always wanted to. He had almost moved to America himself in the early 1930s. A letter survives from a friend who had gone to Boston, inviting him out. Huge numbers from his own area had left for that city when the bleak depression began hitting home in Ireland. The friend wrote that you were as likely to meet someone from home in Boston on a Sunday morning on the way to mass as back in West Kerry. Another letter survives in which the friend makes it clear that times were now just as bad in Boston as they were in Ireland. My father had been due to take the train to Cork and the emigrant boat just a few weeks later. He never made it.

My mother had never contemplated crossing to the 'Fresh Land' or to 'Bright City' as New York was called. She had had a tragic early life in Ennis, County Clare, losing her father and three brothers before her 21st birthday. One brother was killed playing rugby, another died from meningitis, and a third was killed in the RAF at the end of the Second World War. Her father had died of a haemorrhage. She had briefly considered following her remaining sibling, her sister May, to England and becoming a nurse during the Second World War, but her mother's illness meant she had to stay close. Against all the odds, my father had become a schoolteacher, the first in his family, and indeed his village, to get a teacher training college education. He spent his early years traversing several counties, usually on a bicycle, teaching the Irish language which was undergoing a huge revival after Irish independence. His heart was alive to that challenge and he was full of daring during those years as he felt he was playing an important role in creating the new country. He met my mother in Tipperary when she came to his class and they married in January 1946. There is a photograph of them on their honeymoon in Dublin. He is confident, square-jawed, looking the camera flush in the eye as he strides along O'Connell Street, the main thoroughfare. She is more reticent, looking a little to the side, shy perhaps, but very beautiful in a dress that hugs her figure.

On the train to Dublin I met a priest from the diocese, a family friend who was going to Dublin for the day.

'You must be halfway to heaven by now,' he said. 'Your poor father hardly stops between the prayers and the holy water worrying about you and the journey west.'

I laughed, but his words struck home. It was a lonesome journey. The beautiful countryside I was passing through did not inspire an exile's heart for the flight ahead. The blaze of the sun cast its warm rays across the fields. I could see the cows scatter at the train's approach, heavy, beautiful animals, their great clumsy strides eating up the rolling fields as they sought sanctuary from the approaching noise. There are few Irish sights as beautiful. At the airport, sad scenes of emigration, similar to those stretching back generations, were all too evident. Loved ones embraced at the gate. Tearstained parents bid their offspring goodbye. Hard times had come to Ireland again and the planes were filling up. I thought then of those generations who had left by boat, knowing that they would never return, and how tragic that must have been. Parents who never saw sons or daughters again, children who never saw their parents grow old or bounce one of their grandchildren on their knee. In a country where family ties are everything, such partings must have been pure heartbreak.

Many of the emigrants on this day, however, once having bid goodbye to their parents, had a spring in their step as they made their way to the departure gate. It wasn't all about sadness, but about opportunity for a lot of them. I felt much the same way. Jennie was there, as I expected. She was my love, the Donegal woman I had shared my life in Dublin with for about three years. We had met at college and she stood by me during a particularly tough time in my life. We lived together in a little flat in Leeson Street where we played house, like all young couples do. We, two penniless students, had dreams of buying it and settling in Dublin where we would both get teaching jobs and live happily ever after. The dreams melted away because of the heat of my ambition and my disappointment with teaching. I was going to get out.

Jennie was not coming with me. Her heart was in Dublin; the same intimacy and closeness that repelled me attracted her. She loved the craic, the gossip and the eternal backbiting, the friends she had gathered to her and me, because she was far more outgoing. Taking her out of that would have been like tossing a starfish on a rocky shore. She was meant for Dublin. We embraced.

'I love you,' I said.

'I love you too,' she replied, but I knew she had a sense that we would find it tough to overcome this separation. We talked about how she would come over when I had some money put together and she put on a brave smile, but her eyes were sorrow-filled when I kissed her. At last we let go of each other and she strode off without glancing back. She was wearing the same Afghan coat she always did then and I watched as it disappeared into the distance. I was severing my single biggest tie to Dublin.

At the gate I linked up with several friends who were on the same flight. The early morning blues and the farewell to Jennie had now given way to a rising excitement, and, with the arrogance of youth, I quickly forgot those left behind. Like giggling schoolkids, we were all looking forward to this trip into the wild blue yonder. Most were stopping off in New York, some going to points further west or to Boston. We were some of the lucky ones, the first generation, really, that would never be more than a plane flight away from home. For centuries exile had been a death sentence, with few ever coming back. Now it was different. On the plane we drank and talked about how great America would be, perhaps to cover our nervousness. None of the others, as far as I knew, was set on emigration as against a summer fling. Just before take-off a group of schoolchildren from Dublin got on for the trip to Shannon, probably an educational tour. They were wet-nosed and red-eyed from their early morning start and I could imagine the excitement in their homes as they rose and prepared for this trip. I looked at their sleepy little faces and the first pang of homesickness struck me.

At Shannon, the bar and the duty-free store beckoned. I chose the bar and whiled away the waiting period building up my bravado with Dutch courage for the trip ahead. It was a scene I would repeat many times over the next few decades. But I was taken with a sudden fit of melancholy as the furthest islands off the western Irish coast dropped away beneath the plane's wings and I realised that this might be the last time for a long while that I saw the land of my birth or my family. I tried unsuccessfully to sleep, but I was never a great flyer and each dip and yaw of the plane startled and woke me. Far from calming me, the drinking seemed to have the opposite impact as my heart pounded every time we dipped, and I gripped the seat tightly. Finally, over Newfoundland, I got up and strolled to a window at the back of the plane. There I looked out and saw the snowcapped tips of mountains, huge gorges, mighty rivers and as still a landscape as in an oil painting. It was my first view of the American continent.

A fellow traveller, a young priest, was gazing out the window with me. Like me, it was his first trip to the US. He told me that he was on his way to a parish in Florida. He was an only son from Leitrim, an isolated county, and it was soon clear from what he told me that he was his mother's pride and joy. They were small farmers and now his aging father would be left alone to manage the few cattle, the poor soil and the lumpy hills. He had one sister, but she had already left to be a nurse in England. He told me how his mother had dumped an entire bottle of holy water over him at the airport as he left on his first foreign assignment. His father had not come, preferring to stay on the lonely farm. The night before, they had got drunk together, and in the small hours of the morning, the worse for drink, his father had broken down and cried and cursed that he had ever become a priest. 'There will be no one left at home,' he told him. 'I wanted you to have the farm, to raise your children here.' Now that would never happen.

The priest's eyes welled with tears as he told me the story. He was moving to Boca Raton, leaving Leitrim, his parents and the seminary in Dublin far behind. 'It's a lonesome feeling,' he told me. 'Going to live among strangers. I've been told I won't be home for two years. It's enough to make a grown man cry.' I wasn't feeling the most robust myself: too much booze, the late night before, and my mouth as dry as sandpaper from dehydration. My bravado about the prospects for my new life had dimmed somewhat.

Chapter 10

NOT SO WELCOME TO AMERICA

After six and a half hours, the city of New York hove up on our right. I rushed to the window on the other side of the plane, as did many others, to catch a first glimpse. As far as the eye could see there were vast urban landscapes interspersed with patches of green. As we swooped in over Long Island, we could see the long stretch of pristine sand and the Atlantic waves lapping up against the shoreline. Now the airport lay dead ahead, beyond the broad expanse of water. The runway seemed to stretch on forever. A strong crosswind produced a final bump as we approached, and then, mercifully, the wheels touched down so softly that I hardly knew we had landed. Some of the passengers applauded. Six hours and forty-five minutes after leaving Ireland I was in the New World. The sailing ships had taken weeks, the steamers five days or so. I was there in less than a good night's sleep.

The Aer Lingus plane disgorged us amid some heartfelt good-byes and pleas to stay in touch. If there were personal doubts or misgivings we hid them well from each other.

Once on the ground we were directed to the immigration control area. It was hard not to feel intimidated by the sight of the burly agents, hunched over their machines, closely examining every arrival. A few years later, returning to the US illegally, I panicked when I realised I had a business card from my American company still in my wallet. I had only one option as the line snaked towards the counter. I slipped it in my mouth and chewed it, swallowing it with a great effort just as my turn at the counter arrived. I was lucky on that occasion; they asked me to remove the contents of my wallet and I would certainly have been caught. I had heard many tales of people stopped because they had American labels on clothes or a receipt from an American store. There were apocryphal stories too, about carpenters showing up with their work tools in their bag and construction workers with their California driver's license. I knew of one case where a slightly inebriated friend tried to chat up a cute immigration inspector and he ended up back on the next flight home. On this occasion, armed with my valid temporary work visa, the inspector was perfectly courteous. As were the custom officials.

I strolled outside for my first view of the city. The hot breath of a New York summer enveloped me immediately. The temperature was somewhere in the 90s, but the humidity made it feel even hotter. In moments I could feel the sweat gather on my body. Cold winters and lukewarm summers in Ireland had not prepared me for this. In all my life I had never experienced such heat. Despite that, Kennedy Airport seemed somehow familiar to me. With America it is always difficult to separate the reality from the endless movie reel in our heads, but I sensed a familiar yet not known landscape. My attention was immediately grabbed by the sight of the holstered gun on the policeman on traffic duty. Up to that point I don't believe I had ever seen a real gun in my life. Then there were the people, charging off in every direction, a cacophony of noise and excitement and different languages, all combining to produce a frenetic effect. It was exciting and awful at the same time.

Why were such people in a hurry, where could they possibly be going? Little did I know that in a few years I would become one of them.

After an hour or so of sightseeing around the airport, I went to the TWA terminal to catch a flight to Chicago. I was now on the last leg of my journey and surrounded by strangers. The by now familiar pangs of homesickness struck and I found myself wondering what my family and my girlfriend were doing at that particular moment while I was heading away from all of them at over 500 miles per hour. The flight was full of people going back to their homes and spouses. My seatmate was a banker, returning from a business trip to New York.

'You only have to watch one thing in Chicago,' he told me, when I explained that it was my first time there.

'What's that?' I said, my interest piqued.

'The niggers. Be careful where you go and don't ever go into their neighbourhoods. A friend of mine got stuck on the Dan Ryan expressway in a rainstorm and got knifed to death.'

This was surprising talk to me. It was my first introduction to the kind of casual racism that some Americans practise, seemingly without a thought. To my shame I didn't even demur, preferring to study the in-flight magazine and while away the time staring out the window. We were crossing over the Midwest plains. Every so often, city lights sparkled off the starboard wing and the pilot would tell us where we were. The plane pitched and yawed as it hit a turbulent patch. I gripped the seat tightly and hung on for dear life. Two hours or so later we descended into the Windy City, passing over the city itself on our descent. For what seemed like an eternity we taxied on the longest runway I had ever seen. O'Hare Airport was the size of an average Irish city, I reckoned, looking at the gleaming lights that headed off to the horizon. Eventually we came to a stand at the gate and disembarked. As I said goodbye to my banker friend, he pressed his card into my palm and said, 'If you ever need help getting work just call me.' It was the kind of instinctive kindness you will often find from complete strangers in America, even one who swore about the 'niggers' taking over his city.

Once off the plane, I looked for the person from the football club designated to pick me up. Vainly I searched the sea of faces at the exit gate until I saw a large, heavy man with an unmistakable Irish gait come panting up the arrival lounge. It was indeed my contact, a kind soul called Joe Gleeson from Kerry, the Chairman of St Mel's, the club I was to join. 'Welcome to Chicago,' he said, out of breath and looking at me a little askance.

I didn't blame him. I was dressed in my usual outfit: an ill-fitting pair of jeans and a scruffy sweater and shirt, with a straggly beard and long hair. I wasn't big on appearances, in fact quite the opposite. It was a source of pride to me that neatness in dress or appearance didn't matter. I knew he was thinking that this surely wasn't the big hired gun he had paid to come over from Ireland. 'You're welcome to Chicago' he said, again, his voice containing not an inflection of the twenty years or so he had spent in America. It was just as though he had stepped out of his Kerry village on the same flight as I came on. 'Thanks,' I said. 'It's great to be here. We went outside into the warm Chicago night and I could immediately feel the clammy air stick to my skin. 'Don't worry, you will get used to it,' Joe advised as we walked towards the parking lot. 'Even I can stand it now.'

Joe lived in a modest townhouse on Chicago's West Side, a typical suburban residence where Joe could dream of Ireland all night long, as he told me he did, yet live his own modest version of the American dream by day in the construction and furniture business. I was introduced to his wife, Sally, and their two children, Kevin and Sean, who were on their best behaviour for this total stranger suddenly landed in their midst. Exhausted by the long trip, I asked for a beer and made small talk for an hour or so before Joe decided I needed to call it a day. I was completely bushed and couldn't wait to tumble into bed – any bed.

That first night, in a gesture of hospitality that only a fellow Irishman could understand, and despite my loud protests, Joe had his wife sleep on the couch while I slept in their best bed. It was an uncomfortable feeling to begin with, but it became a lot worse when Joe himself climbed into the bed beside me. He lay down and talked to me of 'the old country' as if it were the most normal circumstances in the world. To outsiders it might have seemed like a scenario for a homosexual tryst: two grown men lying side by side in a bed in a darkened room in suburban Chicago. But it was no more than an act of exaggerated hospitality on the part of my hosts.

Nevertheless, I spent my first night in America wide awake, listening to the loud snores of a 300-pound Kerryman. I thought of Jennie back in Ireland, alone in our little flat. No doubt she had the transistor radio on to the pop station, Radio Luxembourg, to help her fall asleep. She always smoked a cigarette and we often lay in bed together watching the arc of the cigarette and humming along to the hits. Just now, that seemed like heaven. I wondered if she was thinking of me.

At some point towards early morning Joe awoke and lit a cigarette, its red glow casting an eerie light across the room.

'Are you awake?'

'I am.'

'It's a great country, America. You'll do well here.'

'I hope so.'

'I just have one piece of advice for you: stick to your own – it's the best way to get along.'

Years later I would read the same advice as it was proffered to Frank McCourt of *Angela's Ashes* fame when he came to the US. Perhaps it was built into the DNA of Irish emigrants everywhere and from every generation.

'I will,' I lied.

'Good man,' he said, extinguishing his cigarette. 'You'll do fine so.' There was silence for a moment and then he said, 'I miss it, the old country I mean.'

The expression was to become very familiar to me in my years in America, but this was the first time I heard 'the old country' used in relation to Ireland.

'I think I know what you mean,' I said, because I was missing it too, after just one night, particularly my warm bed back in Drogheda that I never had to share with a large Kerryman.

'Not a day goes by that I don't think about it,' he told me. 'I still wonder what field they're planting this year on the old farm and what the neighbours are up to.'

'I understand,' I said, although I didn't. Reared in an urban environment, I had no feeling for nostalgia about farm life.

'I wish I was back there.'

'I know.'

'It'll never happen, I suppose.'

'I suppose.'

'Do you know the old Tom Jones song, "The Green Green Grass of Home"?'

'Yes, I do.'

'We'll sing it together,' he said. And so we sang, two men in a bed, our voices softly echoing across the Chicago night:

The old home town looks the same, as I step down from the train,
  And there to meet me is my mama and papa,'

Joe was near tears now, something he was easily moved to.

'... Down the road I look and there runs Mary...'

'Shut up in there!'

It was Sally, trying to sleep on the couch. Obviously this wasn't the first time her husband had decided to belt out a song at four in the morning. We stopped singing. In the silence he lit another cigarette and the glow arced across the room.

'Stay away from the American women now.'

'Why?' I asked.

'They are too smart for the likes of us.'

'Okay,' I said, neglecting to point out that he himself was married to one, and a wonderful person at that. He probably wanted me to continue our conversation but I was too exhausted and soon fell asleep.

I was quickly to learn that each generation of emigrants holds their version of the truth close. Paul O'Dwyer, the happy warrior of Irish America, told me once that when he came out in the 1920s, the emigrants from the 1890s didn't think much of him and his fellow new arrivals. The oldtimers didn't believe the newcomers worked as hard as they had to and that they got it much easier. So it has been for every successive emigrant stream since.

In the last century, emigration from Ireland has seemed to follow a thirty-year pattern. In the 1920s, those who left were the men and women, like O'Dwyer, who were on the wrong side in the Irish civil war, many of them embittered, glad never to return to the partitioned country they left behind. The next tidal wave of emigration occurred in the 1950s: the sons and daughters of small farmers from the western seaboard of Ireland, fleeing harsh economic times. Conservative by nature, many never had the opportunity to further their education. In the main they stayed close to neighbourhood and religion and greatly resented any erosion of either. Then there were the 1980s group, who, like the men and women of the 1950s, were fleeing harsh times. This was a much more dispersed wave, with almost every county in Ireland contributing. These emigrants should have prospered in the new land, but by a cruel twist found themselves victim of the new immigration laws. They were the best educated, but in many ways the most deprived generation, as they could not use their skills in the US until they managed to finagle a green card. Nowadays Ireland's economic woes are sparking an exodus once again, much of it to Australia.

As for myself, once my four-month J-l student visa expired, I would be on my own, illegal in the United States. When you are young such matters don't seem as bothersome, but if I were to face such an uncertain future now, as many still do, it would be nearly impossible to cope.

Joe woke me up by turning on the morning television shows. He gave me a running commentary to demonstrate how much he knew. 'Now we'll hear from the weatherman,' he told me at one point. 'Now they will go back to the news.' And so on. All I could see was a gaggle of fast-talking, slick-haired men and women discussing what seemed to me the most inane topics. Soon Joe was struggling into his construction gear and on his way to work.

When he had gone, I continued my introduction to the great American way as portrayed by television. The advertising seemed to come on every five seconds or so and after a while I grew irritated and turned it off. I went out to the living room where Sally had cooked me an enormous breakfast, the first of many, and she had thoughtfully put the air conditioning on full blast. She knew from Joe's relatives arriving from Ireland that the Chicago heat could utterly defeat many emigrant sons.

In the afternoon Joe returned early from work and took me on the grand Chicago tour. Situated where the endless Midwestern prairies and farmlands finally wash up on the shores of Lake Michigan, it remains the most quintessentially American of cities. We went on the Dan Ryan expressway and I remembered the man on the plane telling me about the person who had been stabbed there. I told Joe about it, and he put his foot to the accelerator until we were back close to home. 'We never had much to begin with,' he said as we neared his house, telling me the tale of rural poverty that he grew up around. I told him how my father had gone to school without shoes most of his young life and that there were fourteen of them in a small cottage.

Paul O'Dwyer once told me about the time his father had seen a local farmer come up the road from the Fair Day, lurching from side to side. 'Look, he's drunk, Daddy,' Paul said to his father. 'No, he's not,' his father replied. 'He wasn't able to sell his cow so he's just pretending to be for appearances sake.'

Chapter 11

TRYING TO FIT IN

Every time I have returned to Chicago since that first time I think of Joe and have the same sense of awe at the city's glistening and seemingly endless skyline from Lake Shore Drive. I have never stopped feeling that there will always be a part of me that calls it home, for it was during my brief six-month stint there that I learnt so much about my new country. That first night it gleamed like a jewel through the heat and humidity and I felt the by now familiar throb of excitement as I contemplated my future there. By the second or third day I was feeling a little bit cocky in my new environment, chancing taking a downtown bus which landed me on Michigan Street in the heart of the city. Sally had given me detailed instructions on how to take the bus and where to go in Chicago but I soon ended up hopelessly lost in the downtown area. I approached a stranger, a woman with shopping bags and a kind face.

'Can you tell me how to get to Lake Street?' I asked her.

She looked at me. 'Is that a brogue I hear?'

'It is,' I said.

'Well, my grandparents were O'Briens from Tipperary. Do you know the family?'

'No,' I said, thinking how there must be ten thousand O'Briens in that part of the country.

'I was over there in 1970,' she continued. 'We had a wonderful time.'

She didn't fit the stereotype, this elegantly dressed woman. From seeing many Americans who came to Ireland, we had the notion that most Irish Americans looked like they just stepped out of a laundromat in Cleveland, with ill-fitting, baggy pants, shamrocks on their caps and probably also on their underwear, and, worst of all, fake brogues. She sent me on my way with detailed directions. I got lost twice subsequently, but the kindness of strangers – putting me on the right road, even offering to take me to the bus station – was a revelation, having heard so much about how Americans were stand-offish and unhelpful. My experience was quite the opposite.

On the second night, Joe took me to meet my new Irish football colleagues, and we were indeed a motley lot assembled in a play- ing field on Chicago's west side. I soon turned out to be perhaps the best footballer there, not for any brilliance on my part, but because the others had hardly kicked a ball in anger since the previ- ous season, twelve months ago. Many had been out of Ireland for a considerable time, some were Americans with only a basic acquaintance with the rules, some were past their playing best when the Summer of Love commenced in 1967 in San Francisco. Paradoxically, the ease with which I was scoring made me aware that this could not be a very good team, given that I knew that the standard overall in Chicago was quite high. It was no surprise to me then, when we adjourned to a nearby tavern after practice, to find out that drinking was a much more favoured pursuit for many of them, and that no one had work or accommodation available to me. I would be staying with Joe for the foreseeable future.

This was a blow because I had heard from so many of my mates at college in Dublin that they had been fixed up with apartments and jobs on their first nights in America. I had somehow expected the same but now felt foolish about it. There were no big construction owners attached to the St Mel's team, just a bunch of workaday folks. Indeed, I soon found out that getting my fare together had probably been a major stretch for them. So I was stuck with Joe and no work. As the weeks went by I got to know Joe as a big loveable mutt, a man moved to tears, alarm or humour easily. His wife, Sally, was a gem of a woman, patient and kind, who never uttered a cross word about the unwelcome intrusion into her home life. Their welcome however, was wearing thin, for them and me. No job meant I was spending hours just walking around the neighborhood or playing with their two children while I was waiting for something to turn up. My teammates were looking increasingly unlikely as a source of help in that regard. Granted, I had not helped my cause with them after the first game of the season.

The night before, we had attended an Irish dance, during which copious amounts of beer were consumed. I was still unused to American beer, but after a bellyful of it I was proclaiming myself well able to handle it – which I undoubtedly did until the next morning. The dance itself seemed a blur. I was a popular man because I was just over from Ireland. Two women asked me to dance, an unheard of occurrence, and I got a little drunker on the strength of it. One of them took pity on me and took me outside, where we sat on a wall. She smoked and I asked her about her life. She was a schoolteacher living in the suburb of Evanston. Her father took her to Irish events nearly every weekend. She loved the 'craic', the Irish word for fun. She wanted to meet an Irish guy and marry him because it would definitely please her father no end. It was all said in a matter-of-fact way, so straightforward that it astonished me. Here was a modern, pretty American woman, and all she wanted was to find an Irishman just like her dad.

My image of American girls had been of 'mall rats' – girls consumed by what they wore, their boyfriends and who was hot right now. A million American movies had convinced me that the last thing they wanted to do was find someone like me.

'Maybe we could go out,' she said between puffs on her cigarette.

'Maybe,' I said as our lips touched and my hand slipped around her waist. She kissed me hard and then I never saw her again. The last sight was of her driving out of the car park in a large Oldsmobile. I immediately loved her.

Greatly fortified by my romantic experience, I stepped back inside and made my way directly to the bar. By the end of the night, as the band played 'The Siege of Ennis', I could barely stand up on the floor. Several women avoided my come-on look as the dizzy dancers stretched back and forth across the floor. I was making a fool of myself and I dimly realised it. I woke up with the worst hangover of my life, accentuated no doubt by jet lag. My mouth was as dry as a desert, there was a fire in my head and when I spoke to Joe on the way to the game I could hear my voice inside of myself. To make matters worse, it was one of those mercilessly hot Chicago summer afternoons, with humidity close to 100 per cent. I stepped out on the field already drenched in sweat and afraid of my life at the thought of the first physical contact, which I felt would probably cause me to pass out.

American Irish football is far rougher than the version played in Ireland and referees are not known for their strictness in applying the rules. In other words, it is every man for himself. I got my 'welcome to Chicago' about five minutes into the game from an American lad, playing the sport of his father but with only a hazy knowledge of the rules. As I came down the field with the football, he delivered a tackle that felt like I'd just hit a shithouse wall. I collapsed in a heap, but foolishly, after a few minutes decided to play on. By now, the ringing in my ears from the tackle had joined with the hammer in my head to provide a symphony all of their own. After twenty minutes I made my way over to the sidelines and beckoned to the coach.

'I can't go on. I'm completely out of it,' I mumbled.

'Listen, son, that is not why we brought you from Ireland. Besides, I have no substitutes,' he replied evenly.

'Oh fuck,' I said.

'Get the fuck back in there and don't be letting down the boys,' he suggested kindly.

And so I went back on, ending up in the corner forward line by half-time, the worst position on the field. I tried to come off again early in the second half but this time the coach was even more blunt.

'I'll have your ass on a plane back to Ireland if you don't stay on,' he threatened.

'I can't,' I said desperately, heading for the bench. I didn't even make it before I began retching, great deep hiccups that caused much disgust to many in the vicinity. 'Get away,' I heard one father bark to his two children, and I had an image of all scattering before me. But I was past caring. All that was important was that I was able to lie down. I lay full length on the ground for the remainder of the game. Figures stepped over me from time to time and there was more than one sarcastic comment. 'Look what they are sending out from Ireland these days,' was one of the nicer ones. What my new teammates felt about this great talent they had flown in from Ireland I will never know, but at least I was spared their commentary in the tavern afterwards by going directly home. There I collapsed into Joe's bed, and a choir of angels, or even Joe climbing in beside me, would not have wakened me.

Chapter 12

BUILDING SITE BLUES

Four weeks into my stay, I finally landed work. It was a measure of my desperation that I took it with a construction company notorious for their exploitation of 'Paddys' like myself, just off the plane. I had no choice, my meagre funds had dwindled away and I was living off hand-outs. In the Abbey bar on the North side a player from one of the other football teams took pity on me and called a friend who landed me the job with Redmond the bricklayer.

'He pays well but is a bastard to work for,' he advised me.

He proved to be exactly right. I started work on a typical Chicago summer day on the city's south side. The heat penetrated everything and sweat formed with the slightest physical exertion. Redmond, my new boss, put me in charge of the mixer, feeding the brickies as they laid the foundations for another batch of 'Micktorian' houses among the decaying structures already there. I knew I was in trouble straight away when he put me in charge of mixing the mortar. Every twenty minutes or so I heard the urgent shout of 'More mortar, More mortar' belching down the wind to the place where I was working. The cry soon began to resonate in my head.

I shovelled each load onto the wheelbarrow. Then I ran with the barrow, a dead run past the serried ranks of bricks, over a narrow defile and onto the gangplank where a slip was fatal. Tip the wheelbarrow there and you were automatically fired. Up to the first brickie, throw down the mortar, then on to the next man, and so on down the line until I had 'fed' four of them. Back then to mixing the mortar and awaiting the next baying call. By ten o'clock I was exhausted and the heat was only starting to rise. Somehow I made it through to the break at 11 o'clock and grasped at the fifteen minutes in the shade. Then it was back to work with a vengeance. 'Shovel or bust' as the construction men say.

Redmond had it in for me from day one, because I was educated, I guess. Fear was a large part of it: anyone who was anyway different, who stood out, was to be feared and belittled. These immigrant men like Redmond had never got anything easy, were used to living by the sweat of their brow and suspicious of those who got the education they never had. I had come across many similar in London where I had worked for summers during my college years. It was a legitimate sense of frustration in some ways, seeing young men coming out with bright futures while all they faced was the eternal mixer, but men like Redmond went far beyond that. Humiliation was his stock in trade.

He came over to me at the mixer, watched me for a few moments and said, 'You shovel like a sissy.'

I ignored it, merely grunting in reply. I had been warned.

'Did you hear me, lad? You're shovelling like a sissy with those soft little hands.'

I felt the anger rise in me, the blisters on my fingers reinforced what he was saying. 'I'm doing my best.'

'My arse you are! You college boys are all the same. Even the narrowbacks can do better.'

That was the ultimate insult, being compared to the Irish American kids, nicknamed 'narrowbacks' because, unlike their fathers, they never had to work too hard. I just had to grin and bear it. For the next four weeks I put up with a daily dose of his sarcasm. At night I dreamt of mortar trays and when I woke up in a sweat I thought I had slept hours when it was only minutes. It was the hardest physical work I ever had to do and the days seemed to be endless. The only respite was a bar called The Blue Fox at lunch time, a seedy place with a pool table and a resident hooker who often disappeared into the ladies room with one of the men. It was heaven, however, for the air conditioning alone, cooling bodies that were raw from the morning sun. Some of the men congregated there after work as well to drink the hours away. It was a sad way to spend your life, one I had also witnessed in London, but it was all they knew.

Strangely, if one of them had been fired, a regular occurrence with Redmond, the other men would not drink with him, almost as if he could spread the contagion to them. It was an example of the fear that Redmond had instilled into them – you could not associate with someone who had angered the boss. Redmond had his spies in the group and could hear everything back the next day. I had seen that type of cowering behaviour in London, too. Many of the construction workers there lived in rooming houses owned by other Irish immigrants who exploited their work and their poverty by cashing their cheques for them, taking a percentage off the top and then charging them inflated rents. Many men worked for the same man who owned their accommodation and who therefore ripped them off on the double.

Years later I read that Irish immigrants in Britain 'on the lump', i.e., paying no taxes all their life, were the saddest of all the retirees, unable to work anymore, broke and often thrown on the mercy of the welfare system. It was not Godless Britain so much as other Irishmen who visited such indignities on them. There are lots of similar stories in America.

Redmond fired me for the mortal sin of showing up in shorts one day. My only workpants had been stuck to me the previous day, a combination of sweat and mortar. I had fallen asleep right after coming home. When I woke up, the mortar had hardened and the pants were as stiff as a board. They could have walked to work themselves. There was nothing for it but the football shorts. As soon as I stepped on the site I knew it was a mistake. The bevy of catcalls that greeted my appearance was led by Redmond who obviously considered such a sartorial breach the equivalent of showing up naked. Why someone could not wear shorts on a building site, especially in killer heat, was never explained to me. It was a rule and when you asked about it you were told to shut up because that was the way it was. Maybe it was against the 'rules', but it was actually the convenient excuse that Redmond had been looking for. He came down to where I was working and jerked his thumb in the direction of the gate.

'You're out,' was all he said. I felt a rush of blood to my head.

'You fucking muck savage,' I said. 'You wouldn't treat a dog the way you treat people.'

He looked at me in complete surprise for a long moment.

'Get out of here, sonny,' he said, raising his fists, 'or it will be very bad for you.'

I threw the shovel at his legs. It missed and he came forward, a grim smile on his face, fists up.

'Now, sonny, let's see how soft you are.'

The scene is still vivid in my mind: the backdrop of the construction site, the Chicago sun high in the sky, sweat pouring down my brow, mortar everywhere. I knew he could easily kill me. He had a mad look in his eyes. I directed a kick at him, aiming for his balls, but he swatted it away like he would a fly. He circled me and I stood still, watching him. I kept trying to kick him, to ward him off. Finally, he grabbed my foot on the upswing and pushed hard. I fell on my back on the mortar tray, the cement clinging to me like a wet blanket. I could feel it running down my back. I pulled myself to my feet. Then I turned and ran. I heard him laugh. Soon all his mates joined in and I could hear the distant echo of their laughter as I hoofed it off the site. My cheeks were red with embarrassment.

For nights afterwards I dreamt that I had stood up to him and delivered a good hiding. In my dream he was on the ground and I was kicking him. He pleaded for me to stop but I was merciless. I now discovered I had made a major mistake. I should not have fought him until I had been paid my last cheque. Back then, three hundred and fifty dollars was a fortune, and of course I never got it. It was a tough lesson to learn.

My next construction experience lasted all too briefly. Soon after being fired, I landed work with a company called World Plumbing that was laying huge pipes in a major construction site in downtown Chicago. To an immigrant, the pay was phenomenal – one hundred dollars a day. It was a fortune and I was determined to hold on to the job. An Irishman called Jim Purcell from Tipperary made sure I had the best shot possible. Patiently he explained the work to me, how to dig the space for the pipes, how to watch above all for any walls of earth collapsing on you, how to lay the length of pipe and then move on to the next part. Jim watched over and protected me on the job like I was his own son.

I was very happy there, taking inordinate pride in hanging out the 'Men at Work' sign every morning, learning to use a jackhammer with the best of them, and joining in the roughhouse culture of the construction trade. Alas, it was not to last. Even Jim's help could not forestall the day when, after a month, the owner, a decent Norwegian man, told me he could not keep me on because of lack of experience. I left, better off financially, but still desperate for a long-term job.

Chapter 13

ANIMAL HOUSE AND FALLING
IN LOVE

C hange came unexpectedly. A member of the St Mel's
football side, Billy McNulty, invited me to stay in his
fraternity house near the campus of Loyola University on the
shores of Lake Michigan on the northwest side of Chicago. It
was summer time and most of the students had departed so I
was able to share a room. Billy was the son of a West of Ireland
man and had remained close to his roots all his life. Having not
yet seen the movie 'Animal House', I had no idea what to expect
when I moved into the TKE fraternity house on Kenmore Drive
not far from the college. I didn't even know what a fraternity
was or what the Greek letters signified, but didn't particularly
care as long as I relieved Joe and Sally Gleeson of the burden of
caring for their overstaying house guest. Paddy O'Leary, a good
friend who had come over from Ireland, also moved in with me
and we had a single room on the second floor of the house.
Most importantly, there were two beds. After sleeping with
poor Joe Gleeson, it was a welcome change.

Because it was summer time, the house was only half full but
that did not prevent the extraordinary culture shock that Paddy
and I underwent. Many of the young men living in the fraternity

house could not have been nicer to the new arrivals, but there were a few utter screwballs who, in hindsight, certainly would not have been out of place in 'Animal House'. It started the first night when sitting out on the porch. One of the TKEs, as they called themselves, arrived outside with a BB gun to shoot at passing tow trucks. We all ducked for cover after his first shots rang out, but, fortunately, I think he missed. The next incident was much more serious. A group of us were walking home from Connolly's, the local Irish bar at the intersection of Devon and Sheridan streets, after a few drinks too many, when we came across an old drunk. He was lolling in the space between two parked cars, drinking some cheap wine. His face told of a lot of hardships and drunken nights, but he was harmless and not bothering anyone.

Without provocation, one of the TKEs hauled him to his feet and began punching him. The tramp was utterly unable to defend himself, having long since passed the point of sobriety. The TKE pummelled him furiously until we got ourselves together sufficiently to intervene and drag him off. The tramp collapsed on the ground, his nose a welter of blood. I blamed myself for not getting involved sooner. Every time I saw the old pug-faced drunk afterwards I felt gutted. It was clear that his nose had been broken in the assault and that his downward spiral had accentuated. The guy who did it was studying to be a medical doctor. It defied explanation. I came quickly to realise that a small number of the young men in the fraternity house were too rich and idle for their own good. It was a syndrome I saw many years later in Ireland when the Celtic Tiger minted millionaires by the barrel load. Aimless young men, bored to distraction with their lives, were fodder for all kinds of mindless behaviour.

It was a new experience for Paddy and me to witness the preening that went on before parties or nights out. In Ireland, a shower was still a luxury item. In Chicago, some of the TKEs spent what seemed like hours bathing and then standing in front of the mirror, looking at their hair and their profiles from every imaginable angle. Then there were the women who called around – beautiful but unattainable to an immigrant like me. I just didn't get it and the harder I tried the worse it seemed. At one house party, a young girl had already announced her intention to sleep with at least three members of the fraternity. I was invited along as an extra to watch. After some thought, I declined.

My best chances were after the Irish football games, when young Irish American women flocked to the Irish bars to meet Irish guys. Here I was a big man, the player out from Ireland, and it certainly made things easier, but I still felt incredibly shy.

'Say that again,' the American women would say when I said something completely mundane.

'God, I love your brogue.'

I loved them too, because they were open and not afraid to engage a man if they were interested in him. They could be wild, too. We went to a late night party where lots of drink and drugs were consumed. I found myself in a bedroom with an attractive blonde girl. We kissed and cuddled and she made it known that next time it could be a lot more interesting. Alas, I never caught up with her again.There is a massive culture gap between America and Ireland. Because we both speak the same language, that difference is often elided, but humour, politics, lifestyle are all quite different, as I soon found to my cost. Jokes considered hilarious in Ireland often fell flat. Ironic humour just didn't work and Americans mainly meant what they said, and were very direct. That was a culture shock to most

Irish, who often have a far more roundabout way of expressing likes or dislikes. It didn't help with the fraternity women that I wasn't aspiring to be a millionaire; that my goal at that time was to just make any kind of a living. The women I met there wanted something more exciting, like an accountant. I couldn't blame them for that but I felt like I was speaking a different language.

It was often lonely there at the TKE house. To make matters worse, Paddy, my only mate, had a girlfriend in Milwaukee and I used to dread every Friday evening when he boarded the bus to meet her. The long weekend yawned, lonely and empty until the game on Sunday and the drunken revelry afterwards. This was not the American dream as I imagined it. I called Jennie a few times. Usually drunk, sometimes incoherent. She was always glad to hear from me. We discussed her coming over, but the conversation always seemed to lead nowhere. I had no money, while she was now holding down a job as a temporary teacher. She even offered to send me the fare home. I refused, my dignity greatly bruised. I had one opportunity to meet someone while at the fraternity house: a waitress in the nearby pizza place who paid me a lot of attention. I could never summon up the courage to ask her out, however. This did not go unnoticed by some of the TKE people, who wondered aloud if I was gay – worse than being a child killer in their eyes. I assured them I wasn't. I was just awkward and shy around their women. I came home one evening to find a large refrigerator blocking the entrance to my tiny room. This was a TKE's idea of a joke, to give me a hard time. Try as I might, I could not shift it. My relationship with the frat boys was going downhill fast. Paddy left to go back to Ireland, so it was pretty lonely. I was also barely working, an odd day here and there in construction.

I called home on a few occasions. My father was quite deaf and I could only talk to him in snatches. Often I just listened while he talked about the latest football games or how I was finding America. When I spoke, he mostly could not hear me. It was frustrating, but still wonderful to hear his voice. To my regret, I never wrote to him, satisfying his curiosity about what America was really like. In the last weeks of his life he communicated with me without being able to hear my responses.

My mother wanted me home. That was obvious from her phone calls, and there were times, especially after the refrigerator episode, that I felt like packing up. Two things stopped me. First, I had no money at all to buy a plane ticket, and secondly, the stubborn side of me was asserting itself. Left to myself, I have the instincts of a loner, particularly in a strange land, and I was quite content a lot of nights to be propping up the bar alone at Connolly's or smoking pot in my tiny room back at the house. My financial situation had again become dire to the point where I was existing on boiled potatoes. Talk about living a stereotype! Once, on a Sunday night I went to an 'all you can eat' place, gorged myself and then tried to slip out without paying. Outside I scarpered as fast as I could, only to run into a Chicago cop car. I was stopped and asked why I was running so fast. Unfortunately, a stranger driving past the restaurant had seen me bolt the building and told the officers where I had come from. I was brought back to the restaurant, where the waitress put me to shame by telling me in no uncertain terms that she was responsible for paying for my food if I didn't pay. I apologised and explained that I simply did not have the money, so the owner put me washing dishes in the back. After about an hour of this I slipped away again, this time taking care just to walk, even though every instinct told me to run as fast as I could.

The date by which I was officially due to return to Ireland was still a month or so off, and I was increasingly thinking of going back, even though that was not my original intent. I could have phoned home for money, of course, but that would have been an unbearable humiliation. The big man who had set out for America boasting about how he was going to make it there would be revealed as a complete idiot. Pride would always stop me making that call. Then it all changed. One of the guys on the football team told me about construction work with a man called Harry Johnston in Evanston, a suburb of Illinois. I called Johnston and he told me to start the following Monday. I practically cried tears of relief. I ran through my last money that weekend and was faced with trekking to Evanston on foot as there was no way I could afford the train fare. I walked seven miles or so to work on the Monday morning, rising at 5:30 in order to make the 8:00 start. The night before, I had plotted the route on a Chicago map, got lost several times, and was delighted to eventually find the coffee shop where Johnston was waiting for me. He was a decent man, of Scandinavian origin, middle-aged, with a silver mane and keen blue eyes, and I will always be thankful to him. He saw right away that I was in need of a square meal. Without a word, he stood me breakfast, but was probably surprised when I ordered second portions of everything, and some soup besides. I was famished. He must have wondered what kind of new employee he had signed up. Seeing my need for food, he reached into his pocket and gave me a $50 loan. I will never forget him for that; it was the equivalent of being handed $1 million at that moment.

After the first day at work there I knew I was off the skids.

Harry's son, Jeffrey, was in charge of the job and we got along famously. Jeffrey was wild and reckless and so was I on our frequent nights out, but he never failed to show up for work, no matter what. It was a good lesson for me, as I joined him on some of his expeditions to single bars. One night he brought me to Rush Street, the main night spot, to a bar where there seemed to be many single women. One of them, a real looker, approached me and asked if I would buy her a drink. Being the dumb immigrant, I was highly flattered and proceeded to buy drink for her all night. I could see the amusement on Jeffrey's face and began to wonder whether I was making a fool of myself. I followed Jeff to the men's room where he told me, 'That's a bar girl. She's there to get as much drink out of you for the establishment as she can. She's paid a percentage of every drink she gets.'

'Why didn't you tell me?'

'I thought you knew. Her vodka is 90 per cent water. Watch the bartender pour it and you'll see.'

'Fuck you.'

I went back, and sure enough, the bartender poured her drink out of my sight and charged me another $5 for it, a huge sum at the time. It was an expensive lesson in how many different ways there are in America to make a buck.

Jeff's friends were as wild as he was. Sometimes we would go back to his apartment in a Chicago suburb. One night, several women, high school friends of his, came around. After much boozing, what followed was as close to a 'love in' as I could define it, with old school friends pairing off all over the place, sometimes in couples, sometimes in trios, except me, of course. I was earnestly trying to expand my own dating horizons. It was difficult and I was not connecting. A peculiar, aching loneliness took hold. I have always found it difficult not to have a woman's touch in my life, but most American women seemed alien to me, didn't laugh at my jokes, or respond to my best pick-up lines. It didn't help that I was probably drunk on a good percentage of the occasions. It was a tough time and I kept harking back to my previous loves, way back to my childhood, and drawing sustenance from the pleasant memories they evoked. It eased the pain somewhat. I would sit in some Irish gin joint and dream about those days.

The first awakening for me was Eilish. She was about eleven at the time and I was younger, probably by a year. We used to sit in Stapleton's field behind my house in Tipperary and talk. We could often hear the corncrake, and once the cuckoo. It always seemed to be summer when I was with her. She loved flowers and I would go and pick them from near the bushes that ran close to the slaughter house. The grass was filled with daisies and she showed me how to make a daisy chain. She laughed, a lovely appealing laugh, when my chain kept breaking. It was hard not to feel a stirring. Once, I took her on a 'date' to the slaughter house that abutted the end of the field. She held my hand as we watched sheeps' throats being slit and cattle gunned down by a big rifle bolt. Then the men would skin the animals and cut the intestines out. We were kids and I was fascinated by this rawness of death.

It was hardly the most romantic of places. Thousands of flies buzzed around the sheep carcasses, the blood washed by us on its way to the nearby drain. The slaughter house men looked massive to me, their aprons stained with blood and grime. They knew me because I often watched them.

'Got yourself a girlfriend, then?' asked one of them as he held the water hose and swept the blood down the nearby gutter.

I went red. She wasn't my girlfriend; the very idea embarrassed me, but I sure was interested in her. She seemed to like me too, enough to go to the slaughter house one more time with me before she politely refused to go any more. It was hardly her idea of a dream date. When she was watching the soccer games that we played in the field, I was always in a lather trying to impress her. I took risks and tackled boys far older than myself. When I scored a goal, I told her it was for her. We sat in the field after the games and I told her about my dreams of America when I was older. She said she thought she might be a nun, because she felt so close to God and one of the sisters in school told her she'd be an excellent one. Once, when she sat cross-legged as we were with a group of friends, I saw up her dress. It was the first erotic moment in my life and I entered a whole new realm. I was confused with the feelings I had for her and there was little guidance or understanding in Ireland at the time. Having bad thoughts was, at the least, a venial sin. So I desperately tried to banish the thoughts about girls, and specifically her, crowding in on me.

Of course our relationship was not meant to last. Her friends teased her mercilessly about me – that I was younger, and that girls needed to go with boys who were older. One Friday afternoon as we sat amid the daisies she told me she wanted to be with another boy 'older than you'. I felt my world collapse around me. It was the end of the affair.

A year later, I was in love again, this time with a nurse from the emergency room in the local hospital. I had hurt my knee playing soccer and she had to dress it. I took my pants off in front of her, the first woman outside of my mother that I had ever undressed for. She was kind and gentle, sensing my unease. She tousled my hair and told me everything was going to be all right. I loved her for it. She dressed my knee and I went home very much the wounded martyr. To my mother and father's exasperation, my knee refused to heal. I insisted that I still had pain, so I could go back to the nurse, which I did several times. She always met me with a mixture of good humour and feigned exasperation.

'Still here,' she'd say when she spotted me in the waiting room.

'Yes,' I'd lie. 'It's not getting any better.'

Sometimes I waited hours for her and refused any other nurse. I knew from their looks and smiles that they guessed I had a huge crush on Nurse Ryan. She had long, shiny black hair and looked like a bright pearl in her nurse's uniform. She was a shining star in my book. Finally, I think my mother realised about my burgeoning love interest – perhaps the nurse told her – and she dispatched me to the doctor, thereby bypassing the nurse. I made a miraculous recovery.

I next fell in love with a nun. I was eighteen years old and finishing secondary school. She was the nurse in the dispensary in the school, still in street clothes, still a novice, and still with questions about her vocation. I was repeating my final year in order to get enough honours to get a grant for college, which meant I was older than the other boys. There were lots of rumours and fantasies about her, as there will always be for any female in an all male environment. She was pretty and petite, with a lovely, kind face.On the first occasion, I went to see her for pills for a bad flu. We ended up sitting side by side for an hour in her cramped office. She told me that the doctor was known derisively as 'the vet' and I should only go to him as a last resort. I liked her. She had a quick sense of humour and a feisty air. She was unlike most of the nuns I knew. Many evenings after that I visited her and we sat in the darkened sick bay, talking about life. I think I was the last disembarkation stop on her way to the nunnery. She loved the idea of the contemplative life. She came from tough circumstances, with much turmoil, and she was looking forward to the calmer water inside the convent wall. Yet she had questions. By entering, she was drawing the veil on her chance of happiness, kids and a normal life.

She talked so softly that I usually had to reach closer to hear her. Once, her hair brushed my face. I could see by her startled reaction that she was taken aback by even that small intimacy. She blushed and I smiled at her. I had an overwhelming desire to put my arms around her and kiss her. It was really not sexual; it was more a protective force, to ward off the lonely life ahead if she was going to follow it. She got up and quickly moved away before I could act on it. As the school year passed it became evident that she was going to go to the nunnery and that the life behind convent walls was her true vocation. I urged her to reconsider. I thought that I might go away with her on an adventure if she agreed to it, perhaps to Dublin or even England. I was thinking of the boarding rooms on Talbot Street in Dublin where a friend had taken his first girlfriend while on a weekend trip to the city. It cost £6 a night, and included a cooked breakfast, he told me, and a landlady who asked no questions. It was the stuff of dreams in fundamentalist Ireland. It also sounded like an impossible dream, and it was. I never asked her.

Soon I was about to leave school for university. She was only months away from joining the enclosed order. On our last time together we walked down the long avenue from the school to the bus stop where I would catch the late night bus home to Drogheda, just seven miles away. It was dark on the avenue, a windy night, and the rustling of leaves made it eerie. On the left as we walked were the playing fields where she told me she walked on her own during the early morning hours. She said she felt closer to God watching the night disappear over the distant hills and feeling the first blush of warmth from the morning sun. On the right were the school walls. Tall and imposing, they ensured that no one could skip out after the front gates were locked. A strange world I lived in: one thousand boys cooped up together, no female teachers, just this solitary nun-to-be. I was afraid even to take her hand in the pitch blackness as we walked towards the road. We stopped under the street light and watched as the traffic whizzed past in a cacophony of sound.

It always seemed to me then that life was what happened somewhere else, somewhere far more important than where I was, and that the cars were rushing to that destination. I was stuck in some unknown place, where not much happened at all. Except her. We stood and talked and I said goodbye to her. Her eyes were soft with sorrow. She answered with a quick kiss, more a brushing of the cheek than anything. Nevertheless I got to feel her soft skin on mine and the touch alarmed me in its intensity. We stood, poised, for a moment. Then in the distance I saw the 11 o'clock bus to Drogheda rolling towards us. The destination was illuminated on the front of the bus, so it loomed larger every yard it drew closer. I was starting one new adventure and she another and the twain could never meet. It was a farewell I would never forget. I never heard from or about her again.

About six months later I lost my virginity. She was a science student, someone I had met at a party. I woke up in the morning to find her stretched across my chest, a mop of hair spread out like a golden star. I stroked her neck and she nuzzled me sleepily. I looked around the room as the sun came up. There had to be four other couples in various stages of undress sprawled around the room. She lived in a small town in the south of Ireland and she had a wonderful look about her, as if game for anything. I loved that wildness in her. She had a flat in Ballsbridge in Dublin. I will never forget the address, and it still causes a frisson when I walk by it all these years later. It was the top flat, which she shared with a college friend. It was just a single room with a shared bathroom down the hall. Like all Irish flats, it was infernally cold.

I was besotted. I would go to the science building and wait outside her lectures, then pretend I was just strolling past. She cooked for me and I stayed over several nights. I felt that I was finally an adult, and that this would last forever. One night, we went out to Howth Head, a mountain promontory just outside the city centre. We seemed to climb for hours until we stood triumphantly at the peak, masters of all we surveyed. The twinkling lights of Dublin lay beneath us. Overhead, an occasional plane roared, en route to Dublin airport. The Irish Sea stretched out into infinity and the reeds and the long grass swayed in the evening wind. In the distance, the Dublin mountains stretched towards Wicklow, the rays of the late evening sun glinting off them down on to Dublin city below.

Then we stretched out in the long grass and tumbled down a hill until we reached the bottom, where we lay, laughing. A man walking his dog came upon us and could not figure out why we were so hysterical. I looked up at the stars, the advancing sentinels of night, and felt this beautiful woman in the crook of my arm, and I thought that this was perfection. We stayed so long we had to walk home. We sang and talked and discussed our families. The road seemed short, despite the distance. I could see the love light in her eyes too. That night would stay with me forever.

I went away to London that summer, swearing undying love to her. After a month or so she came to see me, but, for some inexplicable reason, the love had died. I blamed her brother who had come to visit her while we were in Dublin and soon made it clear he did not warm to me. I thought little of it at the time. Now, however, she was staying with him and it was clear he did not consider me good enough for his adored kid sister. Little by little he succeeded in turning her against me. I fought back, but soon even I could see that his influence on her was greater than mine. I was going to lose her and it almost drove me crazy.

One day she left without a single word and went back to Ireland. It broke my heart. I went into a tailspin, drinking heavily, drowning my sorrows in hotel bars near Heathrow Airport where I was working. Some nights I never went home, just walked around the airport and went back in to my summer job as a baggage handler. For months I could think of nothing else but her. What finally did change everything was seeing her making out with a friend of mine in a corner one night at a party. A rage overtook me and I stalked out. It was the kind of cold shower I needed. I walked home, heartbroken, but nonetheless knowing I had to face the inevitable. I began to heal soon after, but was gun shy about relationships for years.

Chapter 14

GO WEST YOUNG MAN

There was no question about it, Chicago was defeating my best efforts to fit in, and day-dreaming about long lost loves wasn't helping me. Nights at the bar drinking alone only added to the sense of displacement. I longed for a female touch and some interaction. Finally I met an attractive young waitress at a local bar. She took pity on me, I think, as I was often hanging out alone in the corner, reading a book or just staring into space.

She was the typical waitress/acting student, trying to make it in the big city. We plugged in to our common loneliness and shared a love of Irish writing. She was about to play a role in a JM Synge play, 'Riders to the Sea' and in no time at all I was her voice coach. Most of our dates were about helping her with the proper pronunciation of the Irish syllables she was uttering. The play is a gloomy piece about young men lost at sea and the despair and grief of the surviving relatives. She was playing the part of Maurya, the mother of one of the men who is lost. We read the major piece she had to recite over and over. We spoke it aloud. I knew most of it. In a grief-stricken soliloquy in the play the mother realises all is lost: 'They're all gone now, and there isn't anything more the sea can do to me ... I'll have no call now to be up crying and praying when the wind breaks from the south, and you can hear the surf is in the east, and the surf is in the west, making a great stir with the two noises, and they hitting one on the other…'

Her accent was quite good except she didn't understand that the piece had to be read as poetry, not as prose, which is what I always thought Synge intended. I read it to her in a rhythmic way, over and over. She responded. So we sat there on several nights in her apartment, in our underwear, going over the piece again and again. Outside we could hear the busy hum of the city, the fire engines in the distance and the patter of falling rain.

On our last date, just as the play run finished, she kissed me and told me if she ever made it big she would never forget me. She gave me her card and told me to watch out for her name. For years after I looked at the acting credits for Tania Wozniak. I never saw it, though I'm sure she probably changed her name. Some nights, Harry Johnston would call around and drop me home from the job. We would always stop off in his local for a few drinks. When he had one too many, Harry would insist on playing Sinatra on the jukebox and we would listen over and over as the old crooner sang. The bar, full of oldtimers like Harry, would often join in as Sinatra sang, especially for the local anthem, 'Chicago, Chicago' and 'The Summer Wind'. I can never hear either of those songs without finding myself back in Harry's saloon, sitting up at the old oak bar with Sinatra blaring in the background. Johnston treated me so well over the next few months that I was almost embarrassed to take his pay cheques. It was another of the many acts of kindness done to me in America by total strangers like Johnson and Joe Gleeson.

I was officially illegal now, no longer having a valid work visa, working 'off the books', but being an illegal hardly bothered me. It was rarely in the national focus back then like it is now in America and I was just one of many Irish I knew in the same boat. My attraction to America was growing. I told Jennie I was starting to settle in, to call it home. She was upset, as I knew she would be. Ireland was becoming further away each day I grew closer to my adopted home. I loved the bustle of Chicago, the sense of being somewhere important, but winter was coming on, an ominous chill was in the air and I knew the construction work would finish up soon enough. Harry wanted me to stay on over the winter, on indoor work, but I knew it was just a kind gesture more than any particular need he had. My thoughts were turning to warmer climes.

By now, to my great relief, I had moved out of the fraternity house and was living in the apartment of an Irish carpenter named Cyril Power who had been recommended to me by Joe Higgins, a college classmate and friend who later became a fiery, left wing member of the Dáil and European Parliament. Cyril was that rare beast in America – a fully unreconstructed Communist, who believed in the people's right to revolution as much as Americans believed in their Stars and Stripes. This got him into some trouble in his local, where the prevailing sentiment was that Communists should be executed on sight. Because I often accompanied him into the bar, I got dragged into many of the disputes.

One night I got thoroughly drunk, managed to pick up the barmaid, and as we drove home in her car, confessed to her in a fit of bravado that I was a Communist too, despite the fact that I didn't have a political bone in my body at that time in my life. I could see by her shocked expression that I had made a major blunder, that far from impressing her, she was now deeply worried that this atheistic madman in the car with her would somehow infect her. Thus went my first real opportunity of a relationship in America outside the Irish scene. There was also a noticeably cooler reception for me among the bar regulars afterwards. As the winter closed in I began to think more and more of California. The regular work had meant that I was able to pay off the debts I had incurred through loans from friends in the GAA team when I was not working and put some money aside for a Greyhound bus trip. Patsy Mulkerrins, a Connemara man I had become friendly with, told me about his brother in California who would welcome me to play with the Connemara team, known as the San Francisco Gaels, out there. My form with St Mels had improved greatly after my first disastrous outing, so clearly I would have some potential for a San Francisco team, especially one with Connemara connections.

That was the equivalent of finding gold dust. Connemara men were always well connected in the construction business and would look after anyone they signed up. Getting off to a good start in California would be half the battle, unlike what had happened in Chicago. Besides, wanderlust had set in, something almost embedded like a computer chip in every Irish person. To help matters along, another guy from Ireland, Pat Lyne, had told me he was going to go to California too. Pat and I had been good friends in college. I realised it was time to up stakes, cut my losses in Chicago and move on. I bade goodbye to Harry Johnston over an emotional few drinks in his local and soon I was on the bus heading west, my previous lives in Ireland and Chicago gone forever. I was now twenty-five years old.

Chapter 15

A DEATH IN THE FAMILY

The San Francisco Gaels were the local powerhouse football team and took good care of their players. Within a week I was working with Colie Gavin, the captain of the team, who owned his own painting company. A few good performances in practice had convinced them that I was a man worth hiring. The games were played in Golden Gate Park, the huge expanse of green which divides the Richmond District from the Sunset and is perhaps San Francisco's finest feature. The playing field was near Ocean Beach, a stone's throw from the Pacific. At night the famous fog rolled in off the ocean and blanketed the pitch, making playing Gaelic football hazardous. Visibility was often down to ten yards or so and collisions were frequent. We didn't care, we were playing our native game in a far flung field, 6,000 miles from home and it had rarely felt so enjoyable. The cool night air was like a healing balm after the sweat of Chicago. I liked nothing better than to walk from my apartment along the sea front which stretched for a few miles in both directions and listen to the foghorns out on San Francisco Bay.

My joy at my new location, however, would be fleeting. Back in Ireland, my father's health was fading. He had a heart attack while listening to his beloved Kerry play in a major Gaelic football game. My mother described how, as the emergency workers bundled him into the ambulance, he insisted on holding the transistor radio to his ear, and did so all the way to the hospital.

She had known he was not well. Earlier that week, on their way back from town, he had told her to run ahead and open the front door. He was on the verge of collapse when he finally got into the house. Try as she might, she could not get him to see a doctor. He was from a generation where men and women bore their burden stoically to the grave. His own father had lived to ninety-two and had worked every day of his life until he caught a fatal cold and was finally bedridden.

From the hospital, my father wrote love notes to my mother. He signed them 'half a heart' which is how he was feeling about himself. She responded in kind. When he came home he could no longer climb the stairs, so he slept on the couch in the living room. She slept beside him on the floor, often holding his hand in the wee hours when the terror of the night and the unknown took hold.

Years later, when my mother was dying of cancer, she often called out to him during the long nights when it was her turn to be in the no-man's-land between life and death. As she lay dying, she said she felt him in the room and she spoke to him. That was nothing new. After his death I know she talked to him frequently. I often wondered what she said to him, probably in their bedroom, as she waited for sleep. It reminded me of the lines of a poem I had read.

'You are young, you two in loving
Why should you wonder what endearments
Old whisper still to old in bed
Or what the one left will say aloud
When nobody overhears, to the one
Who irredeemably is dead.'

'The living should speak to the dead', she told me once when I asked her if she felt his presence. As she commenced her own long journey after pancreatic cancer was diagnosed, I think she talked with him even more frequently.

So I had hardly arrived in San Francisco when the news of my father's death from the second heart attack reached me. I had been out running that morning, a bright and beautiful day, with hardly a cloud in the sky. I had taken my familiar route, a loop around the lower half of Golden Gate Park, past the Polo Fields where the Irish games were often played, and back to the apartment. When I turned the key in the door I found a group of friends gathered, one of them holding the telegram. I knew it could mean only one thing. I felt faint at the knees. The next few hours were a daze. I had been sleeping on the couch, so there was nowhere to withdraw to, to spend time alone as I desperately wanted. Cup of tea followed cup of tea, but I couldn't face the strong whiskey they kept pouring and offering me. They were kind in the way all immigrants are at a time of trouble for one of their own, but I needed to be with my family. After the initial shock and the frantic phone calls, my father's death left me with a strangely empty feeling. Much of the point of my move abroad, I realised, had been to show him that I could get to make something of myself, after some layabout years. Now he was gone and so was a huge motivating force for me.

Back home, he had woken on the last night of his life and climbed out of his hospital bed to get assistance for a roommate who had taken ill. No nurse responded to his call button and he could find none on duty at the nurse's station some fifty yards down the hall. Exhausted, he somehow made it back to his room and collapsed into bed. The following morning the second heart attack felled him.

As the years have gone by, however, I realise that even though he is dead I am still changing towards him, understanding his own conflicts and insecurities better because many of them are mirrored in my own. Coming as he did from a family of fourteen, surviving on subsistence farming, to make it as a schoolteacher had been an extraordinary accomplishment, and whatever I achieved in my life would be measured against that. I went and sat on Ocean Beach for an hour or more, gazing at the Pacific Ocean, and thinking of the old man. I could not summon up any tears, they would come later.

Strangely, the night before, around the time of his death in Ireland, I had dreamed that he and my mother visited me in San Francisco. He had been dressed as I always remember him, in a tweed jacket, sweater and dark brown slacks. He looked younger than I remembered him and he told me, in between puffs on his ever-present pipe, that everything was fine and that Mom was fine. A message from beyond the grave? Perhaps.

I had to borrow the fare to get home. People were more than kind and I found myself on a British Airways flight to London from San Francisco that night. It was, perhaps, the loneliest night of my life. As we hurtled through the darkness I tried valium and cheap whiskey to settle my nerves, but nothing worked. Because the plane was bound for London, we passed the island of Ireland off to the left hand side. I could see the lights of Cork twinkling in the distance and I found them reassuring in a strange way. Soon I would be home, among those I loved at a time of great travail. I arrived in London groggy and hung over. The valium and drink appeared to be in a running contest as to which was affecting me more. I staggered over to the Aer Lingus terminal, only to be stopped getting on the plane by a British police officer. Just routine, he explained, because of the Troubles. I was so paranoid at that point that visions of being arrested and clapped in irons swam in my head. Fortunately, after I explained the circumstances, he let me go. Soon we were winging our way across the English Channel, the city of Dublin looming up just an hour after departure.

It seemed like I had never been away, but everything had changed in my brief absence. My brothers, Donal, Fergus and Michael met me. Jennie was with them. The men were sombre, dressed in dark suits with black ties. She wore black, too, and I knew she had loved him. They had spent many nights discussing the state of affairs in the North of Ireland, both unabashed republicans who had deeply influenced my own thinking. She had visited him in hospital and had warned me in a letter that he did not seem well. My brothers looked as hungover as I felt. Drink was the great Irish recourse in times of trouble. The sky was as grey as badger skin and rain threatened from the west. All over Ireland people were going about their mundane daily lives, but for us this day was very different. I thought of my mother and her last days with him, sleeping on the floor beside him, caressing him in the dark recesses of the night when he was afraid. She had just left his side at the hospital and returned home when the word came that he had suffered a massive heart attack. She was shocked beyond words.

She was waiting at the front door when we pulled up. She looked gaunt and pale, but her welcoming smile was as warm as ever. 'He talked about you the morning he died,' she told me. It was almost more than I could bear. My sisters, Derval, Triona and Orlaith looked shell-shocked and barely able to cope. It was hard to take it all in.

Later that day I went to pay my respects. His body lay stretched in the mortuary. I leant to kiss his cold forehead and yet found tears would not come. I still recognised this man, but he was now somewhere in a universe far away. I told him that I was blessed just by knowing him. I asked him to take care of my mother and to give us his strength when we faced the hour of our own death. Then they nailed the coffin shut. It was my mother's wish that we all went to confession before his funeral mass. She knew he would have wanted it that way. She had even enlisted the services of Father Peter, a local Franciscan friar, who was a family friend of long standing. I knew it was going to be a disaster. One part of my brain told me to fake it, but I couldn't do that in the old man's memory. To make it worse, it occurred in the living room of my house in the full daylight, so there was no place to hide the flush of physical embarrassment.

'How long since your last confession?'

'Sixteen years, Father.'

Startled, he looked at me. 'You were twelve?'

'Yes, for my Confirmation.'

He looked stunned. At the graveside, under the weight of a sullen, overcast sky, I looked at the six feet deep space my father would be buried in. It seemed so small, yet inviting because he would lie there. I knew my mother must have looked at it and known that this was where she would someday lie beside him for eternity. For a moment I lost my fear of death at the thought of the two of them back together. My mother stood over his grave almost imperiously. The final moment of physical communion between the living and the dead ended when the first clump of clay thudded against the coffin. She broke down for the only time. Still I had no tears. I flew back to San Francisco later that week.

Chapter 16

RETURN TO AMERICA

Painting, like the rest of construction, was a total mystery to me at the beginning. Colie Gavin, my new employer, took it easy on me, confining me to back fences and the rear of houses where I could do no damage. The pay was $5 an hour, enough to make a decent living. The memory of Redmond in Chicago died a quick death as I found myself working for an Irishman who treated me decently, even if he found it a real head scratcher that I could not drive. Nor could I really paint for the first few months. I had a few sorry episodes in that time. My first time trying to extend a 40-foot ladder ended in disaster when it crashed to the street. Luckily, there were no passers-by or they would surely have been killed. Indeed, a kindly old lady watching my antics came out of her house and offered me a cup of tea as a consolation.

'Well young man, you could certainly have done some damage there. You were very lucky. I was watching.'

'Yes, I'm sorry. The ladder got away from me,' I said, afraid she was going to call the cops to remove this incompetent young painter, who was a clear threat to life and limb in the neighbourhood.

'Well, it didn't hit anyone, or any power lines, so don't worry too much about it. Would you like a cup of tea?'

'Oh yes, please.'

I could have been back at home. Another time I was up a ladder when a 5.8 earthquake hit the Bay Area. As the wall seemed to move and the ladder shook, I thought I was suffering some kind of hangover flashback as I had been out very late the night before. It was only when I got to the ground that I realised what had happened and my knees started knocking. The painting allowed me to make a decent wage and to move out on my own. After a few months I moved from Martin Mulkerrin's house to another house on 24th Avenue and Geary, not coincidentally a few blocks from the Blarney Stone bar. The move meant I was now in the heart of the Richmond District, which was my favoured area to live. The Richmond District was later to become heavily Chinese, something that was a major culture shock to me when I returned after being away from San Francisco for a few years, but there was still a strong Irish presence. The neighbourhood ran right down to the Pacific Ocean and was as calm and serene as a country village. Most evenings the fogs rolled in off the sea and blanketed the Richmond in a cool embrace. I loved it; the clime reminded me of Ireland and I could see why so many Irish had come here. Indeed, San Francisco had a great Irish history. From the time of the Gold Rush, the Irish had flooded to the city by the Bay. For many of those Irish it was the last stop on the Continent and the last chance to make it in America. Many found that it was also easier to make a living there than on the East Coast. In the latter part of the twentieth century, the Irish had settled primarily in the Sunset and Richmond districts, built an Irish cultural centre and created their own image and likeness of the land they had never truly left behind.

Initially, there were four of us in the house on 24th Avenue, but then a new influx of emigrants started to arrive. It was the beginning of the exodus from Ireland that started in earnest in the early

1980s, and the immediate impact on us was that about ten people were suddenly living in a modest three bedroom house. Most were like myself – with college educations but no work worth speaking about in Ireland, and had left out of sheer economic necessity. Two had come from Northern Ireland, Catholics fleeing the Troubles. As I got to know these two, I finally got a sense of what it was like to try to live an ordinary life in a state where murder and mayhem were daily occurrences. Neither was political in the Northern Irish sense of the word, but just by their stories and experiences I built up a mental image of the discrimination practised against Catholics there. My father had been a staunch De Valera man all of his life and his trenchant views on partition influenced me. But the Troubles had become so bloody and heartbreaking that it was hard for me to carry the same certainty that he had. My siblings had gone their separate ways, politically speaking. My brothers Fergus and Michael went on to hold office for Fine Gael, one as a TD, the other as Mayor of Drogheda. My sister Derval also worked for candidates for that party. Triona was usually a staunch Fianna Fáil supporter, as was my brother Donal, for much of the time. My sister Orlaith, who had joined me in America, was a nationalist.

Back home in the Republic, while we had watched events unfold in Northern Ireland, we rarely felt part of the Northern Troubles, preferring to overlook the shocking events on our doorstep. Now, for the first time, 6,000 miles from the Troubles, I was experiencing second hand what they were really about. At this distance from Ireland, I noticed for the first time how we were being defined by the Troubles. Often the first topic of conversation when you were introduced to someone new was, 'Why are Catholics and Protestants killing each other?' It defined us every bit as much as the less lethal 'shillelagh and shamrock' stereotype. You found you had to focus on it. Certainly, when I decided to go into the newspaper business I recognised it would be a major part of my job to educate myself about it, as I was being frequently asked to comment on it – usually when there was an atrocity.

What really brought that home was the death of Lord Mountbatten, blown up by an IRA bomb in August 1979 just before I launched my newspaper. The commentary on the event was wall to wall and I realised once the newspaper started up, I would be a source of future interviews on the North.

We were a motley crew in the 24th Avenue house, and one that had their share of disagreements. Given the tightness of the space, that was hardly surprising. At least two of the women staying in the house swapped boyfriends, which led to its own tension. One night I came home to find a brawl going on between the two men and the two women. The cops were called by the neighbours and eventually everyone settled down. Every Friday night was party night. I started off drinking in the Abbey Tavern on Fifth and Geary, work clothes on, often bespeckled with paint, and then wound my way slowly up Geary Boulevard, stopping at every Irish local on the way – and there were several. By the time I got to the Blarney Stone I was usually well looped and liked nothing better than to play some country and western staples on the jukebox and regale everybody around me with sad tales of home. Then it was across the road to Tommy's, the Mexican restaurant, for the usual drunken dinner takeout before going home and falling into bed. As far as I was concerned, it couldn't get any better than that.

Some nights I would try and get a woman to come home with me. One evening I finally 'shifted', as the Irish say, at the Blarney Stone. She was a Jewish Southern California girl, confident in the way that only California women can be. We drove to Ocean Beach, which was deserted. A storm had come rolling in from the west and the rain ran in streamlets down the front of the car. It was also bitterly cold, but we were nice and cosy inside her sedan. Then it turned strange. I suddenly felt my backside heating up. I didn't say anything for a moment or two, but the heat continued to creep up my backside until I felt I was sitting on a hot griddle. I decided not to say anything, in case she felt I was some kind of fool. Was the car on fire somewhere? Not that I could see. And still the seat got hotter. I shifted uncomfortably and she looked over and asked me if I was warm enough now. I told her yes and she flicked a switch. The seat suddenly cooled down. I was immensely relieved and acted like nothing had happened. I would never have thought that a device to heat seats existed. I thought ruefully that they would go down well in Ireland where it is always cold.

We decided to brave the elements and took off down to the water's edge. We watched the wind blow across the waves until they became like white horses galloping to the shore. In the distance we could see the lights of the Cliff House, the famous restaurant which hangs on a promontory out over the ocean. Far away from out at sea the wind carried the sound of a foghorn from one of the many boats on the bay. It made a lonesome sound. Apart from that, only the sound of the passing traffic lanced the silence. What to do? Get wet and cold and embrace right there, or run back to the car? We decided on the former and we fell down on the wet sand. I lay flat and looked up at the angry sky as the rain continued to fall. I felt like joining hands with the black night, lying there forever and holding on to this perfect moment. We lay there for a few moments, kissing. Suddenly we heard voices and saw a flashlight as at least two other couples began to make their way in our direction. We jumped up and ran back to the car, giggling. Once back in the car I got her to heat up our seats again. We met several times after, but no other date had the sheer spontaneity and fun of that first one.

On another night the father of a roommate died and I happened to be at home when the phone call arrived from Ireland. Grimly, I went to fetch the young girl from the nearby bar. As I walked towards it, she rounded the corner with her boyfriend. I had the strangest sensation of watching from above as they walked towards me, laughing and talking. I knew that what I had to impart was about to destroy one person's happiness and end both their times in America. And so it proved. Distraught, she left for Ireland the next day, never to return.

I was drinking too much at the time, a combination of loneliness and giddiness at my new-found freedom. For the first time in my life I was living clear of all family and having to make new friends in a strange city. I had been away before, of course. I had essentially left home at eighteen to go to college and I had been in London and elsewhere, but only for a pre-determined time and always with the realisation that I was returning home. The drinking eased the pain of separation. Many of the Irish I drank with were unfinished souls. Some had spent tough years on the Alaskan pipeline, in a bleak existence and working eighteen-hour days until they made enough money to start a business in San Francisco. They did not scare easily and they had a well defined orthodoxy to their lives. If I cast any doubt whatever on any aspect of the greatness of America, it was bound to start an argument. So I did, quite frequently, with a few drinks in me. Surprisingly, it never really came to blows.

I was relatively well equipped for the task of emigration, despite the drinking, but if I needed any reminding of what happens to those who could not cope, I could find it every night at the bar in the Blarney Stone, or the Abbey Tavern. There grizzled veterans would endlessly play old Irish favourites on the jukebox and remember how good things had been in the old country, before they got falling down drunk. I had a hunch that they would find things very different from the dream if they were ever to return.

Chapter 17

STARTING A NEWSPAPER

My newspaper career started somewhat inauspiciously. I was still working for Colie Gavin, usually with a Cavan native, Mickey Freehill, painting all over San Francisco. Every few days I would accompany Mickey as he made the trek out to the Sunset district, looking for an Irish newspaper at the Irish Cultural Centre. In this day of internet access it is hard to imagine just how deprived we were of basic news from Ireland back then. If Mickey got an aged copy of the *Irish People*, the IRA support newspaper in the United States, he would be delighted because it had the sports scores. I would lap up all the news and information I could from it. Back then, Irish newspapers never made it as far as San Francisco, so the idea of setting up a local Irish newspaper seemed to me to be an obvious one. There was also a huge sea change coming in the community, with a new influx of Irish. Tim Pat Coogan, one of Ireland's leading authors, wrote a book about this period, called *Disillusioned Decades*. In it he explained how the entire Irish economy seemed to come to a shuddering halt after a brief expansion in the 70s. Indeed, between 1971 and 1981 there was net migration back to Ireland as a brief economic boom ensued. By 1981 however, it had all changed. Unemployment had risen to over 15 per cent. The emigrant boats and planes that most people hoped were phantoms from the past suddenly reappeared, like Banquo's ghost. The brief period of inward migration stopped as the planes and boats began filling up again. Heartrending scenes of separation were once more seen at airports and dockside. It was a time of deep gloom in many households throughout Ireland. The problems for the young immigrants who flooded into America in the 1980s, however, were significantly different to those of earlier generations. They were better educated, but changes in immigration law dating from a 1965 Act, ironically passed by Senator Edward Kennedy, ended most European immigration. It meant that most of the Irish who came were undocumented. Women and men with degrees and college educations were forced to take the same kind of work – as nannies, or in construction – as their forefathers. Because of their illegal status they also had no voice to speak to their concerns.It was a strange dichotomy. Though the best educated of all Irish immigrants to the US, they were as constrained as the previous generations in what work they could do because of their undocumented status. Still they came in their droves, seeing emigration as a kindly light amid the encircling gloom of the downfall in the Irish economy. Like homing pigeons, they repeated the traditional patterns of emigration. Galway and west of Ireland people went to Boston, Achill Island to Cleveland, Cork and Tipperary to San Francisco, Mayo and Connemara to Chicago and the Midwest and almost every county to New York, following tracks laid down by earlier generations. The influx into San Francisco revitalised many long moribund organizations. Irish games began to flourish and the original three football teams soon grew to seven. Irish bars began opening up in the old neighbourhoods and the Irish Cultural Centre underwent a transformation. It was in this context that I was thinking of a new newspaper.

I had started my own painting business, Sundance Painting, after learning some basics with Mickey Freehill and Colie Gavin, with my old Chicago friend, Tom McDonagh. Like me, he was keen to try something new. Our new business was barely holding together. Indeed, were it not for William Lu, the kindly Chinese landlord of our recently rented house on 40th Street in the Richmond District, we would have been utterly broke. For no good reason that we could fathom he engaged us to paint all his buildings. Otherwise we would have starved for lack of work. Without any certification or real background as painters we were really up against it. About six months in, I had a narrow escape when some scaffolding I was working on gave way and I very nearly plunged to my death. It was the final straw for me and house painting, and I was determined to build a better career. I needed to keep my feet on the ground.

Driving in the Sunset district with Tom one afternoon, I spotted a store that sported the legend 'All Your Printing Needs'.

'What about this newspaper idea?' I asked Tom.

He looked at me quizzically. 'What newspaper idea?'

'The one I mentioned last week. With all the new Irish here maybe we should start a newspaper.' I said, pointing at the printing shop.

'Ok then,' he said.

Thus are careers in publishing begun. We went in and met a smooth-talking salesman who convinced us that we could start a newspaper for a couple of thousand dollars. We were delighted. I often think back and wonder if he had been honest would we ever have started down the road. Probably not. Between us we scraped together $952 exactly and decided we were going into the publishing business. I knew I wanted Jennie over with me to start

117

the newspaper. She was a great writer and editor and there had been too many lonely nights for both of us. When I called her and asked her to come out, she agreed immediately. She knew, as I did, that this was our last best chance together. When she arrived at San Francisco International I took great pride in showing up in my twelve-year-old Audi, which I had just learned to drive. Things were awkward at first, but the pressure of putting out the newspaper soon consumed us all. I read that 90 per cent of new publications failed. In a fit of defiance I taped it on the wall over my typewriter. Real men didn't fail!

And it really wasn't as huge a risk as it seemed. We were young, unknown, and if we failed we'd probably move on to something else. This wasn't Ireland, where every business venture would be scrutinised, your family history analysed and any failure tantamount to a life sentence against ever starting a new business again. No, this was San Francisco, and if we failed here there was always Los Angeles, or New York, or some other point east or south or north. I think a little of the pioneer spirit of the city had infected us. Having made the decision to start the paper, I resolved to learn to type, not a bad idea for a budding editor. I bought an old typewriter and set to it, hammering out stories from the *San Francisco Chronicle* until I began making a fist of it. On my first night typing, a friend dropped over after football practice. An old construction hand, he seemed almost frightened of the machine, and viewed it with some alarm.

'What the fuck are you doing with that thing?'

'Learning to type. Tom and I are starting a newspaper.'

'Well, fuck me, if that isn't the daftest idea I've ever come across.'

'Thanks.'

I hardly needed to be reminded of the anti-intellectual bent in the older Irish community. The orthodox view was that such notions were better left to their children, and that their lot in life was the hard grind of eternal physical work. It was sad in a way, because many of those I had come to know were extremely bright and focused people who would have benefited greatly from further education. Most, however, had left school in their early teens and hit the pavements looking for work almost immediately afterwards. As a result they had little time in their lives to ponder further education. To a man they wanted their own children to have the benefits they never had, but they had major problems with anyone in their own peer group or younger getting above their station.

College educations were regarded with suspicion and any notion of putting pen to paper was viewed as strange. Indeed, our friend's reaction was one widely shared in the community, as we soon learnt. The notion of a new newspaper when one had not been started in decades seemed an impossible one. But we were willing to buck the odds. And I had form. I had been fascinated by newspapers and writing for them since I was a child. At the age of thirteen I became a horse racing tipster for a community publication in Drogheda. A few years later, I started a school newspaper and then wrote a television column for a new local paper. So it was in my blood, if not in my background, but I had never attempted anything on the San Francisco scale.

Chapter 18

PUBLISHER AND
CHIEF BOTTLEWASHER

The first edition of our newspaper appeared on 14 September 1979. It was all of twelve pages, yet it represented the totality of our dreams, hopes and ambitions. In the first editorial I wrote, 'This newspaper is born out of a hope that we can act as the link between the various strands in the community and strengthen the bond of birth and upbringing that we all can share.'

We called the paper *The Irishman*, after an old San Francisco Irish newspaper. We were, of course, labelled sexist for choosing such a name, but, to be honest, it never occurred to us that it would be an issue – until I went on a local Irish programme in Berkeley, California and spent the first half hour vainly defending it from a feminist presenter. I was young and naive at the time, and it was a fair cop. The newspaper came out at a tough time in Northern Ireland when the violence seemed to be peaking. By now I had spent many hours in conversation with Northern Irish exiles in San Francisco and had read extensively on the subject. I felt that there were no certainties any more, but that some realities had to be addressed and I intended to do that to the best of my ability in the newspaper. American politics had already begun to influence me; I had seen how parties such as the Republicans and Democrats could absorb opinions all the way from the extreme left and right to the centre in their philosophy.

I was also deeply influenced by another emigrant newspaper, the *Irish Post,* in London, whose editor, Brendan Mac Lua, maintained a strong nationalist line despite the mayhem in the North, refusing to demonise one side over the other, but always squarely pointing the finger at the political reality that, like in many other places in the world, such as Iraq, Pakistan, India and Sudan, the British policy of partition had created the problem to begin with.

Mac Lua's was a line I agreed with and I made it clear from my first editorial that we believed that partition was at the root of the problem in Northern Ireland, when 600,000 Catholics had been corralled into a state they did not want to be in and had then been ruthlessly kept out of power for decades. It had not, therefore, been surprising that when political change was not forthcoming, violence had erupted. It would only end with a decent settlement, fair to all sides, and there would be no military victories.

The newspaper launch coincided with my sister Derval's wedding, and I had to assure her in some protracted phone calls that I was really starting a business the same day and could not make it to the wedding. The easier choice might have been to go home and forget about the newspaper, but I had the bit between my teeth and was not about to spit it out. I had worked harder than I ever did in my life preparing the first issue. I found myself driven by a creative force I never knew existed in me. In the month of the launch it was nothing for us to work nineteen-hour days and get up after a few hours sleep and go at it again. It was a pattern that would become all too familiar. Every day brought a new crisis. Jennie was the type never to shirk a challenge and she performed Trojan work. She had the same level of conviction and commitment to *The Irishman* as the rest of us, and, despite the long hours, we were all looking forward to the launch when the day dawned. Then disaster almost struck.

On the way to the printers to collect the first edition, some thirty miles south of San Francisco in a town called Menlo Park, our car broke down and we were forced to try to hitchhike to the printing plant. Hitching on a California highway is extremely difficult, and as the clock crept forward and no ride was in the offing, I became very nervous. Finally a car stopped, driven by an American Indian who insisted on passing around a whisky bottle when we told him where we were headed. He was on his way to Los Angeles to a tribal council. He considered it a good omen to help somebody every day. We were just glad that he showed up.

We made it to the printer just in time to see the first issue going on the presses. I walked into the print room to hear the strains of the theme music from the film, *2001, A Space Odyssey* playing on the radio just before the presses started up. It seemed a harbinger of success. It is hard to describe what it is like seeing your own creation finally come to life for the first time. We had spent all of our $952 on the first issue and were already in debt, as the printer had insisted on being paid up front, but somehow it didn't seem to matter at that moment. As the paper rolled off the presses, with French, instead of Irish harps on both sides of the masthead, it felt like a unique personal creation. I was overcome with emotion and just wished that some of my family had been there to see it. In all the years since, I have never lost that thrill of the press rolling, the smell of printer's ink in the air and the hustling as a new edition of a newspaper flows off the presses.

We led our first issue with the Pope's visit to Ireland, which was just about to occur. It was a huge story back in Ireland but not covered very widely in the American press. Our second lead was the search for oil off the West Coast of Ireland, entitled 'Light of the Emerald Oil'. All in all, we were very happy with the edition. With bundles under our arms and proud as punch, we visited several of the Irish bars in San Francisco that night, showing off the newspaper like a new child. Then we ended up in the Blarney Stone, among our friends, getting drunk in celebration. We were finally on the road. We printed 5,000 copies and it sold for fifty cents. Irish immigrants, especially recent arrivals, were our target market. We distributed through newsagents and Irish bars.

The next morning, reality hit. Jennie and I were hopelessly hungover and we stared at our creation through drink-addled brains. Suddenly this little twelve-page paper didn't look like a very big deal, but we knew what it had taken to bring it out. And now we would have to do it all again, this time with no money. We were stone broke and would not be able to publish the second issue of the newspaper. It looked like we were going to have the shortest lived newspaper in the history of publishing. Then, one of those magical events occurred that made me feel that fate was on our side. Tom happened to have a passing acquaintance with the local doctor for the Irish community, Michael McFadden, a Scotsman who had a large practice in the Mission District. He went to see him, told him the story and brazenly asked for $5,000. Amazingly, Dr McFadden obliged. The death of our publishing venture was staved off and we even had some over to pay for a few staff and office equipment.

Today I marvel at McFadden's generosity to two young guys he hardly knew. Such acts of kindness were not unique to McFadden.

Time and again when our venture ran into trouble we found a helping hand. Joe Finucane, a bar owner in the Sunset district, wrote a cheque for $1,000 when we were desperate for cash. Another time, five local businessmen gave us $2,000 each to keep the newspaper going. Kindest of all was a man called Bill Lewis, our typesetter, who had no Irish blood in him, but was one of those decent Americans who make the country a great place to live in. Each issue we would arrive at Bill's typesetting shop in downtown Oakland, not the greatest neighbourhood in the world, and Bill would treat us as if we were his children. He would help us with design and layout, endlessly correcting our typing mistakes, which were many, and even standing us dinner on several occasions when the paper ran late. We were often unable to pay him on time but it never seemed to matter to him or his wife, Elsa, a German native, who also treated us like family. Often she would leave and arrive back with pizza and French fries for us. It was the kind of generosity that became familiar to us. There is an essential decency in Americans that is actually their best trait. They genuinely wish people well, especially those starting out in business, and there is none of the begrudgery often found in other countries. Perhaps because the country is so vast and sprawling, there is little of that.

An example of this magnanimity happened a few weeks into the newspaper when I secured an interview with the then San Francisco Mayor, Dianne Feinstein (later Senator Feinstein), who had done significant work with Irish organisations. To my chagrin, my tape recorder did not work and my cheap camera refused to flash. She never batted an eyelid at this display of rank amateurism. I eventually ended up taking her photograph without the flash by standing on a chair a few feet from her, and then laboriously hand writing down all her responses, forcing her to pause every few seconds. She must have wondered who let this idiot in, but she never betrayed any annoyance. It is very hard to glimpse this side to Americans from the popular culture which shows up on television or in the movies. After you experience it, however, you understand why they became the greatest power on earth.

With much local support from the Irish community too, it was clear that the new newspaper was striking a chord. As young immigrants began to stream into San Francisco, our fledgling newspaper found its feet like a once shaky young foal. Soon after we started, we received a major boost when local *San Francisco Examiner* columnist Kevin Starr wrote a column praising the newspaper. He wrote, 'The book reviews, essays and editorials assert once again that passionate love of life and language that is characteristic of the Irish wherever they are.'

Two stories got us major attention during our first year. Our big scoop was an interview with mass murderer Charles Manson, which came about in a serendipitous fashion. I owed the unlikely interview to three Catholic priests. I was doing a feature on Catholic prison chaplains in California and had visited the California Youth Authority prison where the worst young offenders were held, as well as Folsom and Vacaville prisons, profiling three brave padres who often put their lives in danger to help inmates. The sights and sounds of Folsom, not far from Sacramento, and made famous in the Johnny Cash prison concert anthem 'I'm Stuck in Folsom Prison', will always be with me. The prison seemed like a huge warehouse, with cells piled on top of each other like cattle pens. It was stiflingly hot and not a breath of fresh air seemed to permeate the building. There was no question in my mind that incarceration in this place could quickly drive a man mad. Father Keaney, from Leitrim, a big bluff man with a thatch of blonde hair turning grey, was one of the few human touches to the prison. On our way across the exercise yard, where prisoner after prisoner was working on buffing his muscles, he was greeted like an old friend by many of them. Still, it was hard not to be frightened by the undercurrent of menace that was in the air.

Vaccaville in Central California seemed little better. This was where Charles Manson was confined at the time, and the chaplain, Father Pat Leslie from County Louth, had struck up a relationship with him. He asked me to come down and see him, and I readily agreed. On a white hot day in midsummer, a friend, Colm McCann, and I made the trek down. The outer gates of Vaccaville were imposing, and once inside one gate you were in an airlock until the guard decided to open the second one. An atmosphere of paranoia reigned. Dante's lines 'Abandon hope all ye who enter here' flashed into my head. I had read all about Manson in Victor Bugliosi's book *Helter Skelter* which chronicled the insane killing spree by members of Manson's gang in the Los Angeles area in the early 1970s. Although Manson himself did not carry out the killings, his robot-like followers seemed to respond to his every whim. Although there were far worse mass murderers than Manson, few seemed to plumb the depth of horror and revulsion that Manson did among the general American populace. His followers had murdered Sharon Tate, the eight months' pregnant wife of Roman Polanski, as well as several other innocent people, in a drug-filled orgy of horror. In many ways, Manson was the perfect contrast to the flower power movement and the summer of love in San

Francisco. Middle America had looked askance at that movement, with its emphasis on free love and sex, and Manson provided the necessary vehicle to attack such new fangled concepts.

Pat Leslie was a quiet man, with the slim build of a marathoner, which indeed he was. He had a low key manner and hardly seemed to know much about Manson's notoriety, or more likely, not to be affected by it. Manson's job in Vaccaville was helping out in the church, quite a change to his life on the outside. I assumed that Father Leslie would stay with me during the interview, but he dropped me off in a little courtyard behind the church where Manson and another man, who I later learned had murdered his parents, sat. I almost froze with fear when Father Leslie suddenly disappeared. Manson was much smaller than I had expected, a tiny man really, and he had a swastika emblazoned on his forehead. A few sentences into our conversation I found him quite mad and rambling, and definitely a complete sociopath. He was a man who could stab you with a knife or hold a pleasant conversation with you and not know the difference. His language was incredibly violent.

Years later I got to know a notorious Loyalist paramilitary in Northern Ireland who was part of the Irish peace process. This man reminded me of Manson in the violence of his language and the constant hate-filled assertions. From whatever dungeons of his mind Manson dragged up his fevered cants, it was clear that here was a deeply disturbed person. What was extraordinary to me was how he had held power over so many people. What seemed mostly gobbledygook to me had deeply impacted many of his followers to the point where they were prepared to kill for him. Manson strummed idly on a guitar during our conversation.

Visions of being clubbed over the head with the instrument raced through my mind. I watched every move he made intently. He fancied himself as a songwriter and sang his latest composition to me: something about the damage being done to the birds and the environment by big oil companies. Coming from a man who hadn't hesitated to direct the savage taking of human life, it was quite an irony. I remained deathly afraid throughout the meeting that he would swing the guitar at me, as it would certainly garner him the headlines he clearly loved. In fact, I was working out my moves if he tried to do it. These mostly included running away as fast as I could, but seeing as we were locked into a small court-yard, that may have been quite difficult. In retrospect, the sight of Manson chasing me around the courtyard might have been funny, but it didn't strike me as remotely humorous at the time. Meanwhile, the guy who had killed his parents seemed unhappy that I wasn't interviewing him. He cleared his throat a few times and tried to get into the middle of our conversation. Manson fixed him with what I presumed was his allegedly hypnotic stare, which looked to me more like a cross- eyed grimace.

'Stay out of this, man,' he said, 'me and the dude have it going.'

The mother and father murderer promptly shut up. I was never as relieved when an interview ended and Father Leslie returned.

Leslie took me to lunch in the prison cafeteria and introduced me around. The sense I had from all the prisoners I met was of essentially weak human beings, unable to control impulses the rest of us are able to keep buried. Almost without exception, they had horrific early lives – Manson was the son of a prostitute and was beaten continuously as a child – and had little chance at life compared to others. Yet there was no excusing the horrific crimes. One rapist explained how he felt unable to stop himself doing it, yet he hardly seemed to regret that he had. It gave him that fleeting moment of power, he explained, that he did not have in the rest of his life. So it was about power, not sex, he explained. Another man, a murderer, thought of himself as an essentially useless individual, but with a gun in his hand felt a surge of power that gave him a deep sense of entitlement to go out and get what he wanted by whatever means. Sitting talking to those men in the cafeteria, I was struck by how there was nothing normal about them. They continued to justify their actions all those years later. It was clear that California has a penal system, not a rehabilitative one, and that the prisoners would be likely to re-offend if released at whatever point in the future.

The tension and fear in that prison were infectious. It was only in the car with Colm driving back to San Francisco that I finally relaxed. I had met the craziest man alive, by many people's estimation, and lived to tell the tale. When writing the article in *The Irishman*, I opened with some lines from a poem, quoted in Norman Mailer's *The Executioner's Song*, that summed up Manson to me:

> 'Deep in my dungeon
> I welcome you here
> Deep in my dungeon
> I worship your fear
> Deep in my dungeon I dwell
> I do not know if I wish you well.'

Although Manson had told me I would become famous for publishing the interview with him, I found it very hard to sell. He was still too violent, too extreme for most publications. Eventually the *Sunday Press* newspaper in Dublin and a German magazine bought the rights.

If Manson was bizarre and strange, the California Youth Authority prison was downright sad. Father Liam McSweeney, who had been a next door neighbour of ours in Ireland, was the chaplain, and as he took me on his appointed rounds it was impossible not to feel depressed by the number of young people who had already thrown their lives away. All under eighteen, many were from very tough and deprived backgrounds that gave them very little chance of a normal future. Now they would spend the formative years of their life behind bars.

The three chaplains I met were remarkable men. A rural Irish upbringing could hardly have prepared them for their mission – saving souls in perhaps the toughest environment on earth. In some ways, though, I believe that their Irish background, with its focus on family and on viewing the whole person in religious terms, helped. Seeing them with the lost and damned souls in California's toughest prisons was a remarkable sight. The gentleness with which they dealt with even the most hardened inmates was a rare touch of balm in an incredibly hostile world. I walked away from the prisons counting my own blessings.

Chapter 19

IRISH 1, MOONIES 0

The second major story we broke was about a young Irish girl named Mary Canning who got caught up in the Moonies when visiting friends in San Francisco. Despite the best efforts of her relatives, she was whipped away to the Moonies residence, some sixty miles outside of San Francisco, near the wine country. It was a common enough occurrence for idealistic young Irish to get snared by the Moonies, who were very active in the Bay Area. I had witnessed on a number of occasions the devastation this caused for families in Ireland. To have a child snatched away thousands of miles from home was a horrific experience. Many never saw their kids again; some returned to their families years later, but were permanently changed. Often we would get frantic calls at the newspaper to publish details of a young Irish man or woman who had suddenly dropped out of sight and not reported in to their families. Many times parents feared the worst: they had been mugged and were in hospital, or even killed. In several instances, however, they had joined the Moonies or one of the other sects that dotted the Bay area. According to one expert on cults, the Irish seemed particularly vulnerable to their influence. Dr Lowell Streiker, author of *The Cults are Coming*, told us that Irish and Dutch kids were particularly susceptible to them.

In this case, Jim Canning, Mary's father, came out from Donegal to search for his daughter. A farmer and a big bluff man, clearly ill at ease in the spotlight, he cut a very sympathetic figure when he appeared on news shows calling for his daughter's return. He was a man out of his element in a city like San Francisco. Yet he had an unshakeable conviction that he would win his daughter back, and his confidence spread to all of us. All the literature stated that the best and perhaps only time to get a kid out from under the Moonie clutches was early on in the process before the indoctrination took full hold. It was also clear to me that the weight of continuing publicity was very important. The Moonies did not relish the constant questions they were getting from the media, and the hope was that Mary would be shaken loose by them, rather than have the bad publicity continue.

The story of Mary Canning had spread like wildfire through the Irish community and there was an immediate consensus that an all-out effort should be made to free her. I chaired a meeting of over 300 people where various schemes to win her back were discussed, many of them not legal. The case had become a leading story on all the San Francisco networks and indeed, further afield, and, because of my newspaper expertise, I was handling the media. I argued for a major demonstration outside the Moonie headquarters in Sonoma County, some sixty miles from the city. I believed that taking the fight to their headquarters and the resultant publicity would be a powerful incentive for them to release her. There were a fair few dissenters from this strategy, some of whom questioned whether I knew what I was talking about. Mutterings about this newcomer to town telling the settled community how to handle things reached my ears. Not for the first time, I learnt to trust my own counsel and ignore the naysayers.

The following Saturday, a motley group responded to my urging and undertook the journey to the Moonie headquarters. Included in the gallant band were several nuns and one priest who had seen the television coverage and had decided to join up. Some of the men, totally unbidden, carried hurley sticks, which, for those who are unfamiliar with hurling, Ireland's oldest native game, are rather like ice hockey sticks. Arriving outside the Moonie compound, about forty of us gathered in a circle and began to chant 'We Want Mary'. After half an hour a large number of Moonies came down to the gate and silently observed the chanting. They were like peas in a pod: preppy young men, dressed in conservative tones, and with neatly clipped short hair, the young women in sensible skirts and blouses. Before long, however, as we raised the decibel level, their smooth facade began to crack. Insults were exchanged, and before we knew it, an all-out altercation began. In the middle of it all were the nuns and the priest, belting about them with a will.

It was probably one of the most surreal moments of my life, and the media clearly thought so too as it led all the news bulletins that night. No one was injured in the fracas and we eventually returned to San Francisco with a deep sense of satisfaction at the media coverage and a feeling that we had struck an important blow. So it proved. The Moonies released Mary Canning the following day and her relatives immediately employed a deprogrammer to help her reconnect with her family. Soon afterwards, they returned to Ireland, where, as far as I know, she picked up the threads of her old life. Our headline that week said it all: 'Irish 1, Moonies O'. It is rare to get such satisfaction from covering a story.

Chapter 20

FAREWELL TO JENNIE

Jennie and I decided to break up. The warning signs had been obvious. She was deeply unhappy because she was out of Ireland. We had some pitched arguments: the lack of any extended family and the relentless focus on the newspaper, which was barely surviving, led to a sense of crushing pressure. She was working in a local Dunkin' Donuts and I was jealous of the attention she was getting from some of the customers. Several police officers asked her out, and I'm sure she was tempted. For her part, she was annoyed with my frequent late nights and my workaholic behaviour when it came to the newspaper, but most of all, she missed Ireland. There are some who can never make the adjustment to strange shores and Jennie was one such person. She loved her native Donegal, to go romping on the beach with her dogs and to come home flushed by the brisk wind, with her excited dogs lapping in her wake. She loved Dublin, too, and she just missed Ireland, period.

Early one morning I woke up and realised that we could not continue as we were. She lay in the bed beside me. I stretched out my right hand and let it fall on her soft shoulder. She stirred and came awake. We lay there in silence for a few moments. She lit a cigarette and the only sound was the soft sough of her breath as she drew the smoke in. She spoke first.

'This can't go on.'

At first I denied that this was the case, even though I knew it to be the truth. It was my typical reaction: trying to smooth everything on the surface and letting the hidden emotions continue to roil away. She was insistent.

'I'm heading back to Ireland.'

Despite myself, a deep sense of relief flooded through me. She had the balls to make the call, not me.

'I suppose it would be best.'

'This is not the same relationship we had in Ireland. I'm like a fish out of water here.'

'I know. But I want to stay here; there is some hunger in me that won't let me go back.'

I reached over and kissed her. She looked at me with those big blue eyes and said, 'I'll always love you.'

'I'll always love you too.'

Thus it ended, with a whimper. She left on the plane a few weeks later and there were many agonising phone calls for several months after. But she thrived back in Ireland, becoming a journalist, and later a highly successful lawyer. She had made the right move.

Chapter 21

FRIENDS OR LOVERS?

With my business partner, Tom McDonagh, I eventually moved into a house in the Richmond District, just a few blocks from Ocean Beach. It was a wonderful place to live. The tang of sea salt in the air, the wonderful cooling fog rolling in off the Bay, and the endlessly perfect San Francisco days. We had a dog now, too. We called him Pub Spy, after a famous newspaper character in Ireland, and I liked nothing better than to take him down to the beach as the sun set and sit on the wall and watch the golden rays descend over the horizon. Pub Spy loved to hunt along the beach. He was a small dog, but seemingly fearless, loving to converse and play with dogs of every shape and size and always having that knowing look after we returned home, as if some important information had been transmitted.

We had created an office in the lower part of the house and we lived in the two bedrooms upstairs. Our little business had expanded to the point where we needed a secretary. That was how we met Julia. She was English and impossibly beautiful – high cheekbones, classic English rose features. She was older than us, at least thirty-two, which seemed ancient at the time. She had come over after a broken romance and had spotted our newspaper ad for a secretary. She came to the interview wearing a sleeveless black dress, which also happened to be low cut. We were bowled over from the start. She had that charming London accent, so different to the upper class, toffee-nosed Britspeak. No other candidate came close. I knew right away we were going to hire her – and that I would fall for her. Her resumé was superb and we were both a little in awe. Where had this vision come from?

She told us briefly about her years working in some of the top law firms in England, the broken romance with a married partner and the flight to America and her determination to start again. She needed the break, she told us, her large eyes welling up with tears. In retrospect, it was a good performance, and one designed to capture the hearts of two young Irish lads making their first ever hire. Because she didn't have a work visa either, the job suited her fine, but she was clearly capable of getting much better. Now she was with two Paddys who still spent part of their days running up ladders and painting houses. Despite my resolution to abandon house painting, I still very reluctantly lent a hand when Tom desperately needed help. It was an interesting contrast.

By the time Julia was with us a week, we both knew we had made the right choice. She simply swept in like a whirlwind, reorganised our bookkeeping, even physically cleaned out the office space and the rest of the downstairs area, which hadn't seen a feather duster for aeons. I suddenly found myself looking in the mirror before she arrived in the mornings, checking my breath after breakfast, making sure I picked the cleanest clothes, even making more frequent trips to the laundry. I tried to act cool and casual around her, but more and more my feelings were starting to show. I know she caught me looking at her once or twice, and I wondered what she was thinking. She seemed to encourage the flirting with both Tom and me. She wore the low cut dress a lot, often sat with her legs crossed and her skirt riding high on her thighs. It took great willpower not to stare from where I was, just a few feet away. She had a lovely way of tossing her head and pulling her hair back from her forehead. There was nothing about her I didn't like.

When she talked to her family in England she would speak in hushed tones. Once or twice I saw the glisten of a tear in her eye. She hadn't been away much in her life and this was a difficult move because her father was ill. Every day she would take her lunch to the nearby park and sit basking in the sunshine, sometimes applying suntan lotion to her arms and face. I drove by deliberately two or three times just to see her, but I couldn't pluck up the courage to ask her if I could come along. Tom and I did not discuss it directly, but I sensed that he liked her a lot too. There was a lot to like. We had never been rivals over women before; he preferred the big busty California kind – the ones he could say goodbye to the next day. I liked European or Irish women mainly; I hadn't quite adjusted to the brash American approach yet.

One night, Julia and I went to dinner and I brought her home afterwards. I was hoping she might say something to me as I stopped outside her door, maybe 'come upstairs for a coffee', but there was nothing. I could see why she probably didn't want anyone to come inside. The house looked dingy and was in a very bad neighbourhood – it was certainly a long way from London's West End. Her poor circumstances only made me want her more. It came to a head on a Friday night when she told us she wanted to go for a drink after work. The sexual tension crackled. We almost knocked her down in our eagerness to go with her. Neither of us was going to step back from an invitation like that. Soon we were cruising down Geary Boulevard in Tom's pickup truck. She wanted a quiet place, somewhere where we all could talk. We found it in, of all places, a Polynesian Bar called Trader Vic's close by the Russian Orthodox Cathedral on Geary Street and 24th Avenue. It had a seedy but exotic feel to it, a faux Polynesian hut with a circular bar and lots of leis and grass hoops about the place.

There were just a few stragglers at the bar and we sat on either side of her. Tonight was going to be *the* night for one of us. A few drinks later and we were carefree with each other. Her skirt was riding high on her thighs again and she regaled us with funny stories about London nightlife and the creeps she regularly met. 'Not at all like you guys,' she said, batting her eyes. Tom and I had reached an awkward juncture. It was time for one of us to leave, but neither of us could bring ourselves to. We didn't know which of us she wanted to be with and she had given no indication of who she favoured. We pondered that for a few more drinks until Tom finally screwed up the courage to ask her.

'Well, Julia, which of us do you really like?'

'I like both of you very much, Tom.'

'Yes, but if you had to pick one of us, who would it be?'

She looked first at him, then at me. 'I couldn't decide. You are both very good people and I like you both a lot. I wouldn't hurt anyone's feeling, but if you want to make that decision between you, that is fine with me.'

It was quite a statement .With that, she went to go to the ladies and make a phone call. Tom and I stared into our drinks for a moment. He spoke first.

'You go with her. She's more your type.'

'No,' I said, 'you go with her. I think it's you she likes.'

It struck me that the conversation had gone off in a very strange direction. Instead of two bulls circling, we were like two sheep waiting for directions. Tom declared that he wouldn't take her.

'I wouldn't want to leave you here alone at the bar,' he said.

It was a very touching moment for me, a statement that friendship was more important to him that just a casual relationship. I, on the other hand, thought I was in love. But even with that, I couldn't cross my friend Tom, especially as he was so generous to me in so many ways. I realised then that neither of us was going to go home with Julia. She came back, sat on the bar stool and waited for one of us to speak.

Tom began. 'Well, Julia, we both like you very much, but we don't think it would be fair...'

She stopped him. 'I understand,' she said. 'I want you both to know you mean an awful lot to me ... but I better go.'

I can't remember ever being as disappointed as I watched that beautiful body walk away from me, perhaps forever. But Tom and I had stuck it out together, in a strange ritual of male solidarity that surprised both of us. It was time to get drunk, share a Mexican meal on the way home and fall into bed, dreaming of Julia's perfect body, which I would only ever touch with my mind, as Leonard Cohen might say.

Chapter 22

A POLITICAL AWAKENING

The longer I lived in San Francisco, the more interested I became in Californian politics. I came from a very political household, where my father, an unredeemed follower of Eamon de Valera, who founded Ireland's largest political party, Fianna Fáil, indoctrinated us very young on the importance of politics. I was soon looking to make a contribution in America. My first lesson in the black art of American politics came in 1981. The Richmond and Sunset districts were represented in Congress by Phil Burton, an old bull of the party who was then No. 2 to succeed the ageing Tip O' Neill. Because the nature of the two neighbourhoods had grown more conservative, his district was suddenly shaky and he had been targeted by Republicans.

The major political machine in San Francisco was run by John Maher, an ex-heroin addict and one of the most remarkable men I had ever come to befriend. He had achieved quite a bit of fame, being the subject of numerous articles, a TV film and a full length biography. Maher had founded Delancey Street – what was then and quite possibly still is probably the best drug rehabilitation centre in America. It began when Maher, a convicted felon and heroin addict, went straight, and began bringing some fellow addicts home to his apartment in an attempt to help them. From that small beginning grew Delancey Street. It was enormously successful. Since its founding, over 10,000 men and women have graduated into society as taxpaying citizens leading successful lives. They include lawyers, truck drivers, sales people, medical professionals, realtors, mechanics and contractors. It was all based on an 'up from the bootstraps' approach. Addicts were often sent to Delancey Street by judges instead of serving prison terms. John also took in many of the lost and troubled souls, such as the homeless and hookers, that no other programme would even try to rehabilitate.

Maher reckoned that Congressman Burton was in trouble and that our newspaper was the perfect antidote for the problem. His analysis showed the Irish in the Sunset and Richmond districts to be the swing vote. The Irish vote was trending conservative, but still grateful to Burton for all the services he had delivered. John believed that an endorsement from *The Irishman* would make a big difference. Suddenly I went from being an utterly obscure editor to centre stage in one of the most hard fought political campaigns in San Francisco history, one that was being watched closely nationwide, because if Burton was defeated it would be a big scalp for the Republicans. It reached its climax for me at a major fundraiser for Burton held in a mansion in the posh Pacific Heights district. On the night, the house was chock-a-block with beautiful people: celebrities, media and other political powerhouses. I was starting to feel distinctly out of place, especially when I bumped into the hors d'oeuvres waiter and he spilled the contents on the floor.

The guest of honour was Senator Edward Kennedy, who, regardless of his currency elsewhere, was still a hero in the liberal enclaves of the United States, and, as the most liberal of all, San

Francisco adored him. I was very excited by the opportunity to meet him.When Kennedy's imminent arrival was signalled, all the movers and shakers rushed from the house to line up on the driveway to greet him. I was hanging back until I suddenly felt a strong pair of hands on my shoulders, and Congressman Burton propelled me through the gathering crowd to the place of honour right outside the passenger door of the arriving limousine. As US senators, congressmen and the San Francisco Mayor looked on, Kennedy stepped out, grasped my hand and wheeled to face the clicking cameras and news reporters. What he made of the shaggy-haired, long-bearded young man, clearly uncomfortable in a cheap suit he had bought the previous day at a secondhand thrift shop called the Blind Baby's Bazaar, he never said.

'How are things in San Francisco,' he asked.

'Fine,' I said.

'How is your race going?'

'Very well,' I lied.

'Well, keep it up. You are a shoo-in,' he said. 'How is Tom doing?'

I had no idea who he was talking about.'Very well,' I said.

'Great. Tell him I will call him.'

I never did find out who Tom was. This exchange was followed by an awkward silence. By now I was hoping someone would come and rescue me. Just then, Phil Burton, having given me my moment in the sun, reached in, followed by a scrum of other politicians. My time in the spotlight was gone, but it was a very convincing lesson that all politics are local.Phil Burton won in a gallop and we endorsed him.

John Maher told me I'd done some good, which was more than most newsmen he knew. I got to know Senator Kennedy well subsequently and he laughed when I told him about our first encounter. I was just happy to experience American politics first hand, an arena that had fascinated me much of my life from a distance. Now that it was up close, it didn't seem all that different from Irish politics in some ways. John Maher could have been a party supremo in any major Irish city, and the experience had shown me that national races turned on minute local issues and that loyalty to the machine was paramount, not just in Ireland, but alive and well in America too. Phil Burton died suddenly a few years later, on the cusp of power, just as he was about to become Speaker of the House.

I became a close friend of John Maher and visited him often in 1982 and 1983 at his office in the converted Russian Consulate residence on Pacific Heights. There, this former skid row drug addict would gaze out at some of San Francisco's most beautiful views as he expounded his always trenchantly held opinions. He could hold forth for hours on an endless array of topics, including Ireland, New York, politics and rehabilitating addicts. Through it all, he would drink cup after cup of coffee, rarely allowing any interruptions. He still walked and talked like the old New York hood he was, and it was fascinating. He was an unreconstructed Irish Republican. When Princess Margaret visited San Francisco a few years after referring to the Irish as 'pigs' during a Chicago dinner in 1977, he arranged for several squealing piglets to be released into the area near where she was staying. I was one of the people roped in to help hold the pigs. Having never spent time on a farm I didn't have a clue; neither did anyone else present. The one I was holding began to squirm, alarmed by the bright lights and flashbulbs. I felt my grip slipping, but everyone else was in the same boat. As the media watched, the piglets took off running down the street, with the cameras in hot pursuit. We never did find out where they ended up.

When the Queen visited San Francisco in 1984, Maher organised 10,000 people to march in protest at her government's policies in Northern Ireland .When the hunger strike deaths occurred in 1981, he had a group of Irish Americans carry mock coffins outside the British consulate in a 'made for television' event that brought huge attention. It was a typical gambit by the media-savvy Maher. He was an extraordinary political powerhouse. On any given day you would find judges, contractors and city officials at his office, all waiting for appointments. He was an Irish boss almost as powerful as a Daly in Chicago, and he relished it. He had major ties to Willie Brown, the black son of a Texas sharecropper who was then the Speaker of the California Assembly, the second most powerful job in the state. Later, Brown, forced out of office because of term limits which did not allow him to run again, became Mayor of San Francisco. Between them, Maher and Brown pretty much controlled politics in the Bay area. A lesser relationship he had was with the Mitchell Brothers, porn pioneers who ran a porn theatre in downtown San Francisco, called the O'Farrell Theatre. Jim and Artie Mitchell were involved in every Irish cause that Maher got them into. It was strange sometimes to see the makers of 'Behind the Green Door' – one of the first smash porn films – side by side with nuns and priests planning Irish protest activities. One major meeting was held in the parlour of the theatre while men in brown raincoats hurried inside. When they were given the location of the meeting, many of the attendees, pargons of the Irish community, knew little of what the O'Farrell Theatre stood for. It was an uncomfortable crowd, to say the least. Strippers and hookers wandered in as pillars of the Irish community blessed themselves. Fortunately, no nun or priest showed up and none of the others went home.

After it was over, Jim invited me to take the tour. The Mitchell boys had a touch of whimsy about them that dulled the hard edge of the porn connection. With some of the girls, we previewed a new porn film they had prepared. The male lead was clearly having problems maintaining his manhood. 'Ah, God help him. I'd love to give him a hand,' said one of the ladies, while the others nodded. It was all I could do not to burst out laughing. The Mitchell Brother saga ended very badly when Jim shot his brother dead after a drug induced frenzy. What had seemed a relatively benign porn empire became instead an ugly mess as huge recriminations followed. However, the theatre remains open to this day.

Maher took me to Fresno, California, to meet one of his heroes, and soon mine: Cesar Chavez, head of the United Farmworkers' Union, at their annual convention. Chavez had been described by Robert Kennedy as 'one of the heroic figures of our time'. When he died, over 40,000 showed up to pay their respects as he was laid to rest on a remote hillside where he had often gone to watch the sunrise. Chavez was born the son of a migrant worker in Arizona. In 1975, Cesar Chavez rallied millions across the US in a boycott of grape growers who were nakedly exploiting their migrant workforce. He insisted on tactics of non-violence and is considered a saintly figure still in the Hispanic community in California. In 1968 he conducted a twenty-five day fast to show his support for non-violence. Through it all, he never took more than $6,000 a year in wages.

The first time I met Chavez was on one of the hottest afternoons I have ever experienced. The central California town of Fresno was festooned with Latino flags and emblems as the farm workers gathered. In the great meeting hall I sat spellbound as speaker after speaker railed against the grape growers and called for support of the boycott. John took me upstairs to meet the great man. When Chavez entered the room he did it so quietly that I hardly knew he had arrived. There was no entourage or trappings of greatness. Yet, after a few moments, I knew that he had an extraordinary, quiet presence. Maher asked me to brief him on Northern Ireland. Chavez listened quietly for over an hour, never once interrupting. At the end he told me he had studied the history of the Irish hunger strikes and asked me two questions: would non-violence work in the context of the North, and was there anything he should do to help? My answers were that non-violence was the siren song of John Hume, one of the great leaders in Northern Ireland politics, and that he could help by just maintaining an interest and contacting Hume.

The second time I met Chavez was in John Maher's apartment in San Francisco in 1985 just when John was beginning to go downhill. I sensed that Chavez knew that and had come to offer advice and counsel. Alas, even the great Cesar Chavez could not help a man bent on destroying himself. John Maher began drinking again, for reasons all too clear to his closest friends. His relationship was not going well and the ghosts that often bubbled to the surface during our conversations were clearly back haunting him. He moved to New York. I will always believe the reason for this was so that he could malinger and die far away from the institution he had created and which depended so much on his inspiration.

In New York he began floundering like a starfish thrown on a rocky shore. I met him frequently, as by then I, too, had moved to New York. He got drunk a lot. He became maudlin and sentimental, remembering his mother and speaking in pain-filled tones about the mental illness that dogged his family, and clearly him too. John was friendless in New York save for a small cadre of ex-San Franciscans who protected him as best we could. It was no easy task. He was often incoherently drunk, and, despite everyone's best efforts, the man who saved so many people could not save himself.

He began sleeping in a construction trailer owned by a friend and had his first heart attack, brought on by the sheer dint of his drinking, soon after that. Even after that warning, his death wish continued. It was a particularly slow and painful suicide by a man who had brought back so many others from a similar fate. Back in San Francisco, John was not so subtly being written out of the script at Delancey Street. After their best efforts to win him back to sobriety failed, they simply jettisoned him. To his eternal credit, he never embarrassed them, even as they seemed to give up on him and forget him. I believe he made a determination that however he was going to end his life it would never reflect on his brainchild or on the people whose lives he had helped save. I had one long and intense conversation with him shortly before he died. It was on one of his good nights and he was talking of the old days in San Francisco. I interrupted him.

'Why are you doing this, fellah?'

'Doing what?'

'Killing yourself from drinking.'

He blustered for a moment, but then gave in. 'Too much pain.'

'John, you have so many people who love you, so many you have saved.'

'Yeah, but you know what happened to Elvis Presley?'

'What?'

'They protected him from everyone but himself. That's me. I can help the world but I have to destroy myself.'

Those words came back to me when John finally died of the inevitable second heart attack, a young man, still in his forties. When I heard the news I felt as many others did – that it was a merciful release for a man who was clearly experiencing massive pain in his life. I believe that there are some people, such as writer Brendan Behan, and my friend John Maher, who find it too painful to be alive and are unable to shake the dark clouds over them that lead to unfettered drinking.

His funeral was one of the saddest I have witnessed. Where there should have been thousands from the ranks of the great and the good across America, there was only a handful of us, and a cheap white coffin, little better than a cardboard box. He went into the ground unlamented by those whose lives he had saved, but I wept at his grave, as did many of his San Francisco friends. I know some who still visit that windswept hill where his body lies. Today, Delancey Street lives on as a monument to his memory that even his detractors can never erase. In the end he did not rage against the dying of the light, but he left behind a beacon of hope for which he will be forever remembered.

Chapter 23

TOUGH TIMES IN
SAN FRANCISCO

As Willie Sutton said when asked why he robbed banks, 'It's because that's where the money is at.' In my case, New York and Boston was where the Irish Americans were at. Small newspapers are not good economic investments in San Francisco, especially ones started with less than $1,000. Despite the kindness of friends and benefactors, we ran into crushing cash flow problems about a year into our existence. It became a race against the bank at times, cashing cheques in bars in order to find enough money to cover cheques already written. It was the kind of stressful weekly pressure that made life very difficult. Publishing was the type of business where you never knew when you went to the bank on Friday if your pay cheque would clear. Often times it didn't, and I spent many a sleepless night worrying about the finances. Rent was often in arrears, and much needed office equipment went not bought because of the cash crunch. It was a shame, because the newspaper itself was finding its stride.

We were breaking Irish American stories that few of the other papers, mainly based in New York, bothered to cover. The 1980 Census, with its finding that there were 40.7 million Irish Americans in the US, was an extraordinary fillip to the community. Yet it had gone pretty much unremarked upon until we revealed the story behind the figures. Likewise, the slow but inexorable growth of Irish American political organizations dedicated to achieving progress in Northern Ireland was missed at first. Because many of these had their rubric outside New York, they were ignored in the Big Apple, centre of most Irish activity. By covering them I saw the beginning of a grassroots community outreach that could and did eventually have considerable political impact. Much of this time, from 1982 on, I was also keeping myself going by freelancing outside the newspaper, mainly for the *Irish Press* newspaper in Ireland, covering whatever I could for them.

I will never forget one news editor there, Paul Muldowney, who gently gave me the only tutoring I ever received in writing journalism. He had infinite patience with the stories I sent him and always conspired to give me big play in the newspaper, even when the story didn't deserve it, because he knew my financial plight. My first story for the *Irish Press* almost landed me in trouble with Irish libel laws, which are much stricter than American ones. It involved an Irish priest who was moved by his order out of his parish house. He alleged that it was because another priest in the house was having an affair with the housekeeper. It all ended in tears, with a court action featuring the priest, Father Liam O' Byrne, now deceased, suing his own order, an extraordinary action by a man who I found to be as traditional in his outlook as the most conservative members of his Church.

I got to know him well during the case and we had little in common. Because of a heavy-handed upbringing where beatings by Christian Brothers in school were a regular feature, I had little enough respect for the traditional Church. O'Byrne loved his vocation unquestioningly and would not have a word said against the old mores. Despite our differences, I fully believed that he was telling the truth. There was something I saw in him that deeply impressed me. There is in the Irish character a trait which bridles at the misuse of moral authority, perhaps because the British sought to abuse it for centuries in relation to their country. Liam O'Byrne was experiencing such a rebellion late in his life. Like many Irish, I have always believed that authority has to be earned, not just handed down by edict. The latter was the case on this occasion and O'Byrne was not about to allow his life's work to be steamrolled under by a church organisation fixated on avoiding a scandal. They had picked on the wrong man to jettison. Where other faithful members of his profession would have bowed the knee and accepted the edict, not O'Byrne. For a man like him to have given his life to an order and then to be treated so shoddily seemed to me an extraordinary miscarriage of justice. He was eventually vindicated when a court found in his favour, but the damage was done to him and his order.

For years afterwards he would rehash the case with me again and again, and it was clear that he had been permanently impacted. For the first time, I saw the havoc that institutions could wreak on an individual who did not blindly follow their edict. The very roots of his religion had been shaken but in the end he was the better for speaking out; to have bottled it up would have utterly destroyed him. Years later, Father Byrne was the prison pastor for Dan White, the man who shot the Mayor of San Francisco, George Moscone, and gay City Supervisor Harvey Milk, in 1978. The story was told in the Oscar-nominated movie 'Milk' starring Sean Penn. I received a few letters from White, who subscribed to the newspaper, requesting a meeting, but I never responded, as it was an inflamed issue, with gays quite rightly up in arms that the man who shot their icon had gotten a wrist slap of a sentence. White committed suicide after getting out of prison.

Despite our ability to break stories, the newspaper continued in dire straits. We would have been in even more financial problems if Tom had not continued with the painting business, without which we could never have survived. Often times I had to turn from editor to house painter to help out on the bigger jobs. This sometimes led to a 'Superman' type existence, starting the day as a house painter in some Mission District Victorian and ending it transformed into a (paint splattered) editor sitting at a typewriter until the wee hours, trying to get a newspaper out. I have several photos of me at the time, taken at Irish events, where it is clear that there is paint stuck to my hair! This must have made an interesting talking point for the local community who knew nothing of my secret life as a housepainter. It was also a time when I was drinking too much. The weekly pressure of keeping home and business together was too much.

One of our mislaid plans at *The Irishman* was to start a Los Angeles section of the newspaper and eventually a Los Angeles bureau. It seemed a good idea at the time; there were large pockets of Irish in L.A. who could provide an extra focus and sales for the newspapers. In pursuit of this ambition, I drove down several times to L.A. during 1983 and 1984 to set up the necessary arrangements. The six hours or so drive down Highway Five was always an interesting experience. Often I got off the highway and travelled through small rural towns which seemed to belong as much to John Steinbeck's era of *The Grapes of Wrath* as to the modern day. There was another route to Los Angeles, far more tortuous, but incredibly beautiful, down the coastal route known as Highway One. The vistas were stunning in many places and the names, such as Half Moon Bay, Santa Cruz, Santa Barbara, conjured up the old Spanish and Indian heritage of the Golden State.

The sprawling city of angels was never my favourite place; getting from one part to another proved to be a nightmare as a missed exit on the massive highways could set you caroming off into unknown territory for an hour or two. It was also too spread out for any cohesiveness in the Irish American community. I quickly learned that Irish radio was really the only way for the community to interact and that a newspaper had almost no chance. Whereas in San Francisco I could frequently walk through the two major Irish neighbourhoods and see vending machines for my paper, there was no such possibility in Los Angeles where the Irish areas were so far flung and disparate that there was no sense of community. There were a few radio shows, a thriving Irish games scene, and many Irish social events that provided some focus for the locals, but, as with New York and Boston, there was a healthy disrespect and suspicion of the other city, and an Irish newspaper from San Francisco was always going to be viewed with doubt in Los Angeles.

However, I did have some extraordinary experiences during my trips to Los Angeles. Once, I attended a Gaelic games tournament and was asked to play with one of the sides in a hurling match, as they were short a player. I lined up as goalkeeper because I had a bad back at the time and could not have handled an outfield position. The game, like so many in America, was bad-tempered and there were many controversial decisions, yet my side, the Wild Geese, were well ahead at the half time whistle. When I returned in the second half I saw some supporters of the opposition team, St Brendan's, standing behind my goals, but thought little of it. As I watched the game being played out, mostly at the other end, I suddenly heard a sawing sound and turned around to see the supporters hacking down the goalposts.

'What the fuck are you doing?' I asked the bigger one who was swinging away with abandon while I tried to keep an eye on the play on the field.

'Fuck off,' he said before running away with the posts.

This was clearly their way of expressing disapproval with the game's inevitable outcome. I hardly had time to react when the St Brendan's side mounted one of their infrequent attacks, and I will always remember the face of the forward on their team who bore down on goal, looked up to shoot, then suddenly realised there were no longer any goalposts to shoot at, except for two small wooden stumps. The referee wisely abandoned proceedings right after that. Irish newspapers got hold of it and it made huge headlines. That same night I went to a post game dance where I had to take some painkillers for back pain. This should have warned me off the drink for the evening. Unfortunately it didn't and I was soon slugging back the pints and watching some Irish dancers perform before the dance proper started. I always found Irish dances in California very enjoyable: a mix of old songs and dances like the Siege of Ennis and the Walls of Limerick, some country and western airs and a good dose of patriotic Irish ballads. In contrast, the young ladies present were thoroughly modern Californian women, often with high paying jobs and careers. The dances straddled the generations. Older Irish men and women who hadn't seen 'the old country' in thirty years would dance the sets side by side with Valley Girls singing along to 'Don't Cry for me Argentina' which was big at the time. There was always a raffle to benefit some immigrant without health insurance who had landed in hospital. Often times the older Irish brought their daughters along, hoping they could make an introduction for them to some nice young Irishman. As one father told me, he and his wife were 'petrified with all the drugs and all that' about who their daughter would end up with. If only they knew how much casual drug use there was among the immigrant Irish community, they would hardly have been as anxious to pair up their daughter with an Irish man. In San Francisco in particular the hangover from the Hippy 60s was all too evident, even in the Irish community where pot and cocaine were freely available.

On this particular night, I was apparently in flying form for much of the evening. I say 'apparently' because I don't remember any of it. The first thing I recall is waking up on the floor in my friend Frank's apartment in Santa Ana with the sun shining directly on my throbbing head and realising that there was someone lying beside me dressed in bright colours. Through the fog of an almighty hangover I barely dared to look. When I did finally lift my head I saw a beautiful Irish dancer, in her mid-twenties, still in her full regalia – all bright buttons and shimmers and even the hair piece intact – sleeping soundly on my crooked arm. Draped over us both was a large white table cloth. 'Oh Jesus,' I said. She moaned and turned over, but thankfully did not wake. How she and I got there I will never know and I have no idea what transpired between us. I never got to find out either. I carefully extracted my arm from under her neck, leaped up and bolted into the bedroom where my friend lay sleeping. Soon afterwards

I heard a banging and shuffling and realised that she had woken up and gone home.

Another night, while on a Los Angeles trip, I went to a céilí in Orange County. I danced with a young woman whose parents came from Clare. I told her that my mother was also a Clare woman. Within ten minutes her parents were over, inviting me to their table. When we sat down they regaled me with stories of the old country and what the old days were like in California. The young girl looked on, and it seemed to me she was sizing up a potential suitor. Next came the invitation to visit the house the following night for some dinner. I went along with this, for reasons of loneliness as much as anything. Three thousand miles from Ireland it was nice to get Irish hospitality as I remembered it and occasionally longed for. The mother took over on the second evening, plying me with food and drink until she had squeezed every available iota of information out of me, including whether I did my own laundry. I must have failed the test of the mother as I was not invited back.

The old time waltzes and Irish set dances in an age of disco and loud music must have appeared passing strange to the young girls at these dances, but in a way it was exotic and was as close as they would get to recreating their parents' world. Native-born Irishmen, still relatively thin on the ground, were very popular with such women, and the more countrified the better, it seemed. I saw some strange marriages in my time between West of Ireland men and Valley Girls, not to mention Belfast men, who were very popular for political reasons, to aspiring actresses and models. Athletes were also popular and the then annual visit of the Irish All Star hurling and football teams to San Francisco and Los Angeles were occasions of wonderful sin. Many marriages came out of brief liaisons between Irish football and hurling stars and local women in the two cities. Strapping country Irishmen and the perfectly tanned California girls proved irresistible to each other. After my Irish dancer experience I never mixed booze and painkillers again.

In 1982, I began another relationship, this time with a journalist from the *Washington Post* who had been covering Irish issues from the capitol for the *Irish Press*, the same newspaper in Ireland that I worked for. We carried on a long distance friendship for many months before I flew to Washington to meet her. She brought me to the newsroom of the *Washington Post* and introduced me to legendary reporter Bob Woodward, the equivalent of meeting Muhammad Ali for an aspiring boxer. The *Post* newsroom looked just like the movie set from *All The President's Men* and it was one of those rare times that I had to pinch myself to make sure I was really standing there talking to Woodward. Even then I was not easily impressed with 'celebrity', but Woodward and Carl Bernstein had exposed an extraordinarily corrupt web spun by Richard Nixon, the president of the United States, and forced him out of office in the process. The problem, however, was that within months they had imitators everywhere in the US, all of them looking for the next great breaking story. The long term impact was that journalism became more and more a game of 'gotcha', to the detriment of solid fact-based reporting.

She also brought me to the White House on a VIP tour and it was a very special moment to gaze at the unoccupied Oval Office and meet some key members of President Reagan's staff. I even got to witness the president arriving on the South Lawn. He looked just as tall and leathered as he did on television. She visited me in San Francisco, and, once again, I found myself strolling on Ocean

Beach with a beautiful and interesting girl. We were very keen on each other but it was proving too difficult because of the distance involved. She wanted me to move to Washington but I could not see any future there, and besides, New York interested me far more. We broke up with little recriminations on either side.

Soon afterwards, I met Patricia Harty, who became the rock in my life in San Francisco. There were no fewer than fourteen kids in her family from outside Nenagh in Tipperary, and most of them had ended up in California. She had come via the Bronx where she had written part of an unpublished memoir called 'The Only Other Virgin in the Bronx' which accurately described life in the early 1970s in the most Irish borough in America. She was a typesetter and very good one, so before long she began working for *The Irish-man*. Her value to the newspaper was immense. Soon we were playing house together, in a two-storey dwelling we rented in the Sunset District within sight of the ocean. I loved it there and look back on it as among the happiest times of my life. At night I would run down to the breakers and jog back, taking in the sheer calming beauty of the most delightful city on earth. I remember once, after taking my usual run, lying in the back garden on a bench and saying to myself, 'This is as good as it gets.' I was delighted at what I had built in California: a stable relationship, my own company and a lifestyle far removed from what I had at home.

I went back to Ireland in 1983 for my brother Fergus's wedding. On the surface, it all seemed the same as when I had left, four years earlier, but, of course, people's lives had moved on. Friends had got married and were distant. The hometown, apart from the family gatherings, was full of old ghosts and remembered times. Seeing my father's grave for the first time in four years was also a shock. Instead of his presence, there was a stone slab with his name in Irish and a space for my mother when she passed over in the future. It shocked me to see his name emblazoned on the headstone. Somehow a part of me expected him to be waiting by the front door when the cab from the train station arrived, excited to hear all the news of America. Instead there was a grey stone in a cold graveyard on a driving wet Irish day. A host of memories came flooding back and I cried more on seeing his grave than I did upon learning of his death. During the visit, I took my first trip in many years to West Kerry, his native place. Because I had no immediate memories of the place, it was the best part of the visit, to walk the roads that generations of my father's family walked, to sit in the local pub and listen to the musicians, to walk up by the Three Sisters, headlands that reach out into the hungry Atlantic to form a natural promontory that provide one of the most beautiful vistas in the world.

As we sat in the local pub, my first cousin told me the family story of the Famine and the young woman who died. The family was half- starved and too weak to carry her to the graveyard so she was buried in a field on the land where my father grew up. Padraig made it sound like it had happened just a few weeks previously, so vivid was his account, and it was hard not to be emotionally affected. I also had a personal memory of the lasting impact of the Famine, a fact that often made me realise just how close an event it was to all of us in Ireland, even though it was 150 years ago. My grandmother, my father's mother, who was born in 1871 and died, aged 92, in 1963, lived with us when I was a child. She habitually wore a shawl, and I remember how she would always hoard potatoes under the shawl, as though they were gold dust. No other